My New Rich Life

REDEFINE SUCCESS...
BUILD A LIFE WITH PURPOSE

Matthew Wireman

My New Rich Life

Redefine success. Build a life with purpose.

Matthew Wireman

© 2025 by Matthew Wireman. Published in the United States by OfftheWire, LLC—www.MatthewWireman.com

Cover design: Joel Smith and Matthew Wireman

Interior Design: Matthew Wireman

All rights reserved. No part of this book may be reproduced by any mechanical, photographic, or electronic process, or in the form of a phonographic recording; nor may it be stored in a retrieval system, transmitted, or otherwise copied for public or private use—other than for "fair use" as brief quotations embodied in articles and reviews—without prior written permission of the publisher.

The author of this book does not dispense business advice. He only offers information of a general nature to help you in your quest for business and personal success. This book is not designed to be a definitive guide or to take the place of advice from a qualified professional, and there is no guarantee that the methods suggested in this book will be successful, owing to the risk that is involved in business of almost any kind. Thus, neither the publisher nor the author assumes liability for any losses that may be sustained by the use of the methods described in this book, and any such liability is hereby expressly disclaimed. In the event you use any of the information in this book for yourself, the author and the publisher assume no responsibility for your actions.

www.MatthewWireman.com

This book is dedicated to my amazing wife and four incredible children.

I am a better person because of your love, grace, persistence, patience, kindness, perseverance, joy, laughter, acceptance, and desire for your own growth.

You bring fullness to my life and I thank God for the privilege it is to be your husband and dad.

Thank you is insufficient...but it is begins to get at my immense respect and overwhelming love I have for you.

May you be blessed with the words and teachings in this book...

TABLE OF CONTENTS

Prologue 12

What is the RICH Life? 18

Riches that Last 26

It's Time to BE Better 38

The Rich Mind 48

The Rich Body 76

The Rich Soul 104

Boundaries Make You Free 140

Your New Rich Life 148

Prologue

If you're reading this, I know you get it. I know a ton about you already. Because I'm the guy that reads the Prologue. I know you picked up this book because you're constantly trying to get better. That's why I put it in the subtitle. I wanted to capture your attention. Yes. I wanted you to pick up this book. Yes. You. It's called a filter in marketing. Essentially, I only want people who are serious about personal growth and willing to change to read this book.

I'm sure the book was sitting next to some other self-development book on its left. I am sure on its right was a spiritual healing book of some sort.

This is as it should be.

You see, this book…indeed, my life's mission is to bridge the gap between the spiritual and physical. To help people see that their insides are directly tied to their outsides. Well, not literally, but you get the idea (at least I hope you do…nah, I know you do because you and me are tight!).

I LOVE personal growth. I love the people in this space. I love the vision they put forward. I cut my teeth on everyone from Tony Robbins to Brenden Burchard and did what any self-growth person would do. I went back to their sources. You see, I'm a researcher by nature. I know this got on my parents' and teachers' nerves. Not only did they tell me, but I could see it on their faces when I asked "Why? Where did you find that out?" I did that all the way back to Mrs. Wilson (who I also had a crush on and was crushed when she didn't return for maternity leave… that's for another book!)

I love the people in the personal growth space. They're serious about getting better. As they often say, "Progression not perfection." I need to be reminded of that every day. I have a tendency to beat myself up. You too? You see, I knew it! I look at where I'm at and where I want to be, and I often get frustrated. If I'm not careful, this can spiral down into depression and constant agitation. I can't see all the progress I've made. I can't see that I am in the top level of my profession as a university dean. I can't see that the church we started is in the 20% that don't fail in the first five years. I can't see that I have four amazing children and a wife who is, honestly, my best friend.

It's so hard to see when your vision of success is skewed.

This book is for me as much as it is for you.

I need this book to remind me *what's* important and *why* it's important. I forget…every day.

While I love the people in the self-development space (the folks on my left), I found that book after book, keynote address after keynote address, podcast after podcast, was missing something. I mean, I am talking about dozens of books. Hundreds of keynote addresses. Thousands of podcasts. After all this information, there was one HUGE gap. All of these self-development gurus would talk about the importance of meditation and the spiritual life. BUT they never took the time to help with breathing exercises and sharing that you need "me" time. Both of these are important. BUT there is a plethora of practices that are tried and true to how you can actually form your spirit—aptly called spiritual formation.

I understand. I say this and am sure your eyebrows are raised (remember, I know you!). Too many times spiritual things go into the "woo woo" phase and never get to solid, simple, actionable steps. I don't have time to sit and breathe for an hour. I don't have the kind of lifestyle (nor would I want it) where I sit for hours on end.

I was put here to effect change in the world. You were created by God for a purpose. You know it. That's why you picked up this book.

I want to guide you.

I've been mentoring men and women for over twenty years. I've been doing it for free that whole time.

It wasn't until I got a coach who told me, "Matt, you gotta stop doing this stuff for free! What you have to give to the world I would pay for. It's solid. It's rare."

It took about a year for me to agree with him.

This book is the fruit of that wrestling. I will share more of that in the book.

For now, I want you to answer one simple question: "Do I really want to change?"

Don't breeze over that question. And don't assume that you do. If you're like me, you're quick to say "Yes!" But if you look at your actions, is there alignment? Have you read book after book. Listened to talk after talk, and feel like you're in the same rut?

I think it's largely due to four things: Lack of Direction, Neglect of the Body, Unclear Spiritual Guidance, and No Accountability. I will be dealing with each of these four hurdles in this book and give you clear, simple, and actionable steps to make a change. You know it's time. It's time to be better.

Let me speak plainly. I was asked the other day what this book is about. It took a moment to answer because this book touches on the major elements in our lives that often are talked about, but very seldom integrated.

I thought of myself as a college kid. Full of energy but lacking direction. Everyone seemed to have their opinion, but never really engaged with me as me. They gave the typical answers of working hard and climbing the ladder. Particular to me, though, because I was gifted at leadership and loved Jesus, I was encouraged to go into full-time ministry.

I wish someone would have taken the time to listen to my heart. To ask questions. To push back on my assumptions. To challenge me in love to consider other options that I couldn't even see. I wanted to be a faithful Christian…and people assumed that ministry was the answer.

I wish someone would have given me the time to dream and the space to consider how I was wired.

Now, I'm grateful for my path…but I do also wish someone would have spent the time to help me consider all parts of me that make up, well, me. My mindset. My health and diet. My spirituality. My gifting. My passions. Had that happened, though, I wouldn't have written this book. And I can't help to think that you would be helped too by the lessons I've learned and am still learning.

God has created us as physical and spiritually integrated beings. We hurt ourselves when we only tend to one and not both. You must remember that you have a physical body and a soul. They inform and shape one another.

You also need to remember that you have been meticulously knit together so that there is and never will be someone like you on the earth. God put you here to enjoy his world and bring help and healing and hope and your unique personality to shape and influence this world for this time in its history.

I wish we could have a coffee together and sketch out your story and what the next chapter could be for you. Suffice it for now to read and do the exercises in this book.

And maybe one day we'll get to sit down and have that coffee!

Matthew Wireman
January 27, 2025

What is the RICH Life?

If I were to ask you how you would define the word "rich", I wonder what you would say.

Go ahead. Write your definition down… [Btw, unlike other books, this is a book that is intended for you to engage with. Write in this book. Commit even now to do the exercises and APPLY what you're learning about your world and yourself. If you do this work, I PROMISE you will be a very different person than what you started out as in reading what you're reading right now.]

"Rich" (*yep, go ahead and write it down*):

I would wager that your definition above had some reference to money in it. That's alright. We live in a world where "rich" is synonymous with money...so it's expected. But did you know that the word comes from the Old English word meaning "strong, powerful, great, mighty, of high rank"? It was also used originally in Celtic and Germanic tribes to mean king or kingdom (the word *reich* should ring some bells of kingdom and conquest).

It was over time that strength was reduced to gold and silver because of the wedding of ideas between a king and his being rich in monetary wealth.

In going back to the original, I believe it's helpful to consider for a moment that anyone can be strong and mighty and powerful. This is not reserved for some trust fund babies.

In fact, because we are created by God, who is the King of all the earth, he intended from the beginning in the Garden of Eden that his people experience abundance. He gave them every. Single. Thing in the Garden, except one tree—the Tree of the Knowledge of Good and Evil.

This was not a cruel test or driven by some ego trip on God's part. He wasn't withholding a good thing because he is a control freak. Rather, he wanted Adam and Eve (and us) to look to him to understand what is truly good and evil. This was actually a good thing to withhold.

You see, we are finite and dependent creatures. We are always in a place of need. We need oxygen. We need food. We need water. In having us embrace our boundaries, God is kind to us.

Can you imagine if someone held a gun to your head and said, "You have to fly or I'm gonna cut off your legs." It'd be ludicrous. To expect finite people to do something they can't. It's a burden too heavy to carry. It's a crushing weight.

Trying to determine life on our own terms is a crushing weight. We are not only dependent, but we are constantly learning. It is in God's grace that we don't decide what we want to be at 5 years old. I changed my mind no less than a dozen times! How about you?

This is why being kicked out of the Garden was also gracious. Yes, it was a judgment for disobeying...but had we been able to keep taking from the Tree of Life and live forever without a boundary, we would be undone.

I mention this because in order to understand who you are and where you're going and what you really want in life...you have to know your origin story.

Remember Lambert the Sheepish Lion? Maybe not. Well, there's a story of a lion cub who accidentally got enveloped into a sheepfold. He learned how to be a sheep. He was loved by the sheep. He even tried to bleed like a sheep, but couldn't. He was downcast because he wasn't like the sheep.

Little did he know that he was created for power and strength.

One day, there was a wolf who crept into the midst of Lambert's sheepfold. He was getting ready to have a grand old time at an all-you-can-eat buffet. But right then, out of the depths of who he was created to be...Compelled by love for his family...he roared.

You, too, need to know where you came from in order to know your purpose and meaning.

You were uniquely created by God for this particular time and in your particular geography so that you might experience strength and might. As a child of the King of the Earth, God wants so much more for you than simply existing.

He wants you to claim your birthright as an heir of his Kingdom.

You were created for a Rich Life.

So many of us spin our wheels running after money because we haven't been shown the bigger picture of why we exist. It's nice to have a brand-new car. It's comforting to have a large house and yard. It's more enjoyable to have money in the bank account than seeing $0.

But if you take a moment to consider your origin story, I think you'll find a bigger purpose and meaning.

That's why I am writing this book. To help you see greater vistas than what our culture and world tell us is greatness and strength and riches.

Your life does not consist in what you *have*...but in who you *are*.

Of course, to be a king entails having monetary means. But a king can still be a king even if he is bereft and bankrupt financially. Imagine a king who is in prison by his enemy. He doesn't cease to be a king, does he?

Of course not, he remains a king because it is his birthright. It is who he is...not what he has.

It is, however, not ideal because left in a place of poverty, he will have nothing to leave his heirs. This has happened numerous times in the world, hasn't it? Kingdoms rise and they fall. It's a fact of life.

But a good and true king maintains his financial means, while also being a good governor and servant of the people. To be a good and true king, he must also be a servant. Too often, the world has drawn a line between the haves and have-nots, as though what they have is the determining factor of their value as a human being.

This couldn't be further from the truth.

Your value is not built upon a foundation of what you have. You have to let that sink deep into your bones, my friend. You were created by an Infinite Being to experience a rich and abundant life. And this cannot be equated with mere financial riches.

You may have picked this book up because you were intrigued by the title and the concept of living an integrated life.

The foundation of a rich life is understanding your inheritance as a child of the King.

The principles and practices laid out in this book start with this presupposition. Without it, I believe, we are left flailing and groping about in darkness trying to find the doorknob.

If you look at the underlying problem in the world today, I believe it is due to creatures seeking to figure it out on their own. There's a lot of rancor in our culture right now against religion due to past hurt. Unfortunately, many write off religion of one brand (for example, traditional Christianity) and opt for a different religion (for example, naturalism) of their own making. In the end, this will not satisfy the longing for the transcendent we are all wired for.

To be rich is to step into your purpose and meaning you were designed by our Creator to manifest in your life in the world at this time. So much of popular spirituality tells you to look inside to find your meaning. It is true, and you will see it in this book. We need to spend time in understanding how we are particularly wired and what makes us tick. We need to grow day by day in our own self-awareness…so that we can bring our true selves into the world around us.

Where modern spirituality falls short is that it can often simply stay in the internal. Yes, there are attempts to reach outside of our interior life in talk of meditation and breath work. But we don't merely speak into a void when we pray or cry out in our moments of despair, "Why is this happening?" We are grasping for the Other. The Transcendent. Truly, you and I need a voice from outside us to tell us who we are and why we are here.

It started with parents. Extended to aunts and uncles and teachers and employers…Over time, we bought into a narrative that is still only finite in its foundation. We need a Voice from outside that is Infinite and sees the world as it is so that we can know our role in it.

Like Shakespeare knew the end of his play to the beginning and all the minor movements and soliloquies that would happen, so also God has written a grand story and invites you to see your script, rehearse it, embody it. The real power, though, comes when we so enmesh ourselves in our role that we are able to ad lib when life inevitably happens.

What do I mean? Well, have you ever been to a murder mystery dinner theater? There is a general script and direction. At intermission, they take a survey of the audience and ask them who they want to have done the murder? The actors then act towards that end in mind, all the while staying in character…not needing a script at that point and being told what to do.

So it is in the deepest places of our lives. Like a child, we need to be taught a, b, and c. Over time, we are able to form words on our own and then sentences and then ideas and arguments.

So much of our inmost being needs to be taught and then guided.

This is where many religious folk get it wrong. They don't do the inner work of knowing their coping mechanisms and habits. That is, they don't get to know themselves. As a result, they simply do what they're told.

When they do find a sense of freedom, they can react against those strictures and opt for a deconstructed reality. It is the re-construction that is often the harder part. A part that many never get to. Like I tell my students I have taught for over a decade, it's really easy to critique; it's more difficult to construct.

In Your New Rich Life, I am going to have you dig deep into who you are and how you're wired. I'm going to go through exercises I go through with my clients.

I know, without a doubt, if you slow down and tend to your soul, you will reap true success.

Why do I say, "true success"? Well, just like "rich" has been minimized and equated with a certain kind of riches, so, too, has "success". Too often, the world defines success by external factors: salary, home renovations, how many vacations you take, where you go, what you wear…Even as grown adults, we have not strayed too far from the elementary playground, have we?

Success is becoming what you were made to be.

Read that again.

Success is becoming what you were made to be.

How do you have true success, then, if you don't know what you were made for?

You can't.

That's why I wrote this book. To help you do the hard heart work to find out why you were made and what is in alignment with who you are. This will determine how and why you will achieve success.

My earnest prayer for you, my friend, is that you would indeed be rich in relationships, in mind, in soul, in body…and when these are in alignment, money will come. But that is really only a consequence of doing the hard work.

Sure, there are wealthy trust fund babies who have not done the work, and the financial riches came. I can promise you, unless they have done the work that I am going to have you do in one shape or another, they are not truly rich. They are probably listless or bored or wandering around wondering what they are doing here.

I want so much more for you, my friend. I want you to be tested and tried and purified through hard interior work so that your exterior consequences come.

Let's get started!

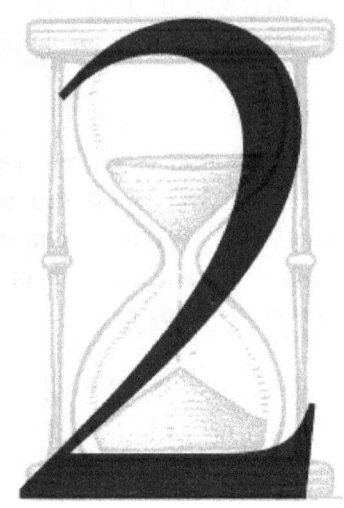

Riches that Last

I'm not sure where it started, but there is a strange phenomenon within religious communities that believes it is evil to be wealthy. They teach that if you get money, then you have compromised your faith. They take the Apostle Paul's words and twist them. Paul told his young protégé Timothy, "for the love of money is the root of all kinds of evil" (1Tim 6.10). People have, unfortunately, shortened the teaching to be "money is the root of all evil."

[NOTE: Word to the wise. Short sayings rarely capture the depth of reality. They allow us the ability to have the appearance of depth but keep us floating on the surface of superficial living.]

What is more. One of the things I teach people as an educator and pastor is that we must work hard to read in context. That is, it is unwise to take a pithy phrase without looking at what was said immediately before or after...let alone in the entire letter (in this case). In fact, it is downright dangerous. I have seen it in others...and in myself. Let me explain this passage a little bit so that we can understand. Are you ready for a mini seminary class?

The entire verse reads: "For the love of money is the root of all kinds of evils. It is through this craving that some have wandered away from the faith and pierced themselves with many pangs." Note that the phrase says, "all kinds of evils". In other words, there's a qualification. It is not "all evil" but "all *kinds* of evil". There are certain evils that are produced without the love of money...but then, you may ask, what does "the love of money" mean? Great question. He gives further contours to it when in the next sentence he says, "It is through this *craving* that some have wandered away from the faith and pierced themselves with many pangs." So he equates "love" with "craving". The word in the original Greek that Paul wrote in has the meaning of "stretching out" or "extending oneself". In other words, the person who stretches himself out to acquire money. You know this person. They reach with all their energy to get one more dollar. You may have been that person. I know I have!

You know what happens when you stretch yourself out? You become vulnerable. Your ability to defend yourself is lowered and you can easily succumb to outside pressures. Take, for example, a powerful boxer. When he attacks and makes a haymaker of a punch, he stretches himself out with all his energy to make contact with his opponent's face. It is at that stretching out his velocity and force is at its highest...but it's also at that same point that he is the most vulnerable. If the opponent can wait and dodge, he is able at that very point to be most likely to actually knock out the one punching. His ribs are exposed. His guard is down.

In stretching ourselves out, we are not only our most vulnerable, but we are our most foolish. How? We have forsaken all the fundamental teaching of boxing by keeping our guard up and keeping our elbows in and patiently waiting and jabbing until the right moment to land the haymaker. So also in life. How many times do we see the wealth of others and opt for the get-rich-quick scheme so often peddled by marketers? We buy into the lie that we can get rich if we just do this one thing. "Wealth gained hastily will dwindle, but whoever gathers little by little will increase it" (Prov 13.11).

But you have to take Paul's teaching in its broader context. Not only does Paul talk about "craving," but then he also talks about "wandering from the faith." In other words, those who love and crave are prone to wander from the fundamental principles and guidance of the Bible. To wander is to forget your bearings and lose your pathway.

But then consider how Paul instructs his young mentee in the rest of the letter. He tells him to "flee these things" (love of money and craving money and wandering away) and "pursue righteousness, godliness, faith, love, steadfastness, gentleness." He tells him to flee external validations for his existence and to cultivate the interior life. His very soul.

But are these things mutually exclusive? Do you either have money or have righteousness? Can we have both? The answer is very clear a few sentences later. He instructs Timothy (and this is SO key): "As for the rich in this present age, charge them not to be haughty, nor to set their hopes on the uncertainty of riches, but on God, who richly provides us with everything to enjoy. They are to do good, to be rich in good works, to be generous and ready to share, thus storing up treasure for themselves as a good foundation for the future, so that they may take hold of that which is truly life."

What are the rich to do? They are to develop the same interior life that Timothy is to do. They are not to be haughty. Positively put, they are to be humble. They are not to put their hope in earthly riches that can rust, lose, and be stolen…but they are to place their hope in God. They are to be rich in good works. And here's the kicker for our purposes at this point: "be generous and ready to share". And by being generous and sharing with those in need (note the "thus"), they are storing up treasure in heaven. Have you ever thought it ironic that God inspires us to action with riches? There seems to be something very embedded in the human condition that God seems to appeal to. Indeed, he re-directs and re-defines what are riches worthy of your time and effort.

Someone may say, "Matt, I'm tracking with you but what about that Rich Man Jesus told to sell everything?" This, after all, is the passage that St. Francis of Assisi famously, upon hearing it one Sunday, was compelled to take a vow of poverty. And it's the passage that generations of Franciscans have cited as foundational to taking their vows of poverty.

In fairness, if you're a Franciscan and you're reading this (chances are very low!), what I am about to say will not persuade you. There is an entire worldview you subscribe to that I will probably not be able to persuade you out of…nor is that my aim. Instead, I am writing for folks who are not compelled to take a vow of poverty. But they may feel a bit of discord or cognitive dissonance in their quest to live a rich life and this very stark call to sell everything they have to follow God. Well, it's like I did for Paul's famous directive, I want to do for Jesus.

The passage in the Bible is in Matthew 19. I will quote it at length here to help bring context to it:

And behold, a man came up to him, saying, "**Teacher, what good deed must I do to have eternal life?**" *And he said to him, "Why do you ask me about what is good? There is only one who is good.* **If you would enter life, keep the commandments.**" *He said to him, "Which ones?" And Jesus said, "You shall not murder, You shall not commit adultery, You shall not steal, You shall not bear false witness, Honor your father and mother, and, You shall love your neighbor as yourself." The young man said to him,* "**All these I have kept. What do I still lack?**" *Jesus said to him, "If you would be perfect,* **go, sell what you possess and give to the poor, and you will have treasure in heaven; and come, follow me.**" *When the young man heard this, he went away sorrowful, for he had great possessions."*

The primary question this wealthy man had was how he might live forever. Now there is debate among people of faith as to what is happening here. Jesus makes it clear that if this man wants to live forever, he needs to do something. Over the centuries, though, theologians have been at pains to say that we can never earn our salvation. This isn't exactly true. At least, not according to Jesus. If you and I want to have riches that last forever...Indeed, if we want to live forever, we simply need to keep the commands of God. After all this, was God's promise to Israel when he said that in keeping? After a long re-telling of the Law of God, Moses said, *"For it is no empty word for you, but your very life, and by this word you shall live long in the land that you are going over the Jordan to possess"* (Deut 32.47).

Right before this, Moses also said: *"For this commandment that I command you today is not too hard for you, neither is it far off. It is not in heaven, that you should say, 'Who will ascend to heaven for us and bring it to us, that we may hear it and do it?' Neither is it beyond the sea, that you should say, 'Who will go over the sea for us and bring it to us, that we may hear it and do it?' But the word is very near you. It is in your mouth and in your heart, so that you can do it.*

> **See, I have set before you today life and good, death and evil. If you obey the commandments of the LORD your God that I command you today, by loving the LORD your God, by walking in his ways, and by keeping his commandments and his statutes and his rules, then you shall live and multiply, and the LORD your God will bless you in the land that you are entering to take possession of it.** *But if your heart turns away, and you will not hear, but are drawn away to worship other gods and serve them, I declare to you today, that you shall surely perish. You shall not live long in the land that you are going over the Jordan to enter and possess. I call heaven and earth to witness against you today, that I have set before you life and death, blessing and curse. Therefore choose life, that you and your offspring may live, loving the LORD your God, obeying his voice and holding fast to him, for he is your life and length of days, that you may dwell in the land that the LORD swore to your fathers, to Abraham, to Isaac, and to Jacob, to give them.*
>
> — Deuteronomy 30.11-20

Jesus is simply picking up the words and teaching that stretched all the way back to Moses before Israel entered into their Promised Land. But something very persnickety is embedded in this teaching. Did you notice it? There is a condition in both Jesus' and Moses' words. Did you see it? I emboldened and italicized the key dialogue to make it more evident. A condition is something that must be met before what follows can happen. Jesus said twice, "If you want eternal life," then "keep the commandments," and "sell everything and give to the poor."

Now Jesus truly meant this for the young man. He was able to peer into the heart of this young man and see that he had been faithful in many things, but he still lacked the very heart behind the obedience. That is, he was using obedience as a justification for him to be owed by God.

He had the condition reversed. He, rather, needed to have God at the center of his life and the motivating force behind his actions and then obey. Jesus knew that this young man's true God was his wealth. And that's why he commanded him to crucify that idol in his heart so that he could truly honor and revere God.

As a good rabbi, Jesus is simply pointing the man to the teaching handed down generations prior by Moses. I also emboldened and italicized the relevant verbiage from Moses to make this clearer. He says that God's people are able to obey God.

He is not asking them to do impossible things. He is not asking them to fly or to hold their breath underwater for an hour. He has given them the faculties to be able to do what he tells them to do…so that they might live long in the land…which is a picture of eternal life. I don't have time to get into this, because it will take us too far astray from the purposes of this book, but I simply want to say that the Promised Land was a reminder of the Edenic Paradise which is, in turn, a beautiful utopia of heaven…aka, life with God.

Back to the point. Moses tells them people that they have the physical ability to obey God. He wants them to have life and have it abundantly (see also Jesus' words in John 10.10). How do they obey these hundreds of commands? Simply *"by loving the LORD your God, by walking in his ways, and by keeping his commandments and his statutes and his rules"*. We often hear the word "rules" and we tighten up. It's okay. You can relax now. The idea of rules is actually a very gracious and powerful thing in the Bible.

The myriad of gods that were offered at that time did not give clear rules that had been written down. If you wanted to know what Ba'al had to say, you had to go to the local priest and he would tell you. And what you had to do was largely dependent on the kind of day the priest was having, whether he liked you or not, or whether he had some bad wine. You did not know from one day to the next what your god required of you. The key difference between those tribal deities and the God of the Bible is that his ways are written down so that not only you know what to do, but the priests are also held to account for how they live and direct the people.

Okay. That was quite a bit. I appreciate you sticking with me. That may have been something new for you—walking through a text of the Bible…but I believe it is foundational for how we are to know how we can have riches that will last forever. To put it another way, to have eternal life…or to have an abundant life.

We have two other places to go as we lay this foundation of what it means to have a truly rich and abundant life. But before we do, let me finish up Jesus' teaching about the rich young man. After the young man went away, we read:

And Jesus said to his disciples, "Truly, I say to you, only with difficulty will a rich person enter the kingdom of heaven. Again I tell you, it is easier for a camel to go through the eye of a needle than for a rich person to enter the kingdom of God." When the disciples heard this, they were greatly astonished, saying, "Who then can be saved?" But Jesus looked at them and said, "With man this is impossible, but with God all things are possible." Then Peter said in reply, "See, we have left everything and followed you. What then will we have?" Jesus said to them, "Truly, I say to you, in the new world, when the Son of Man will sit on his glorious throne, you who have followed me will also sit on twelve thrones, judging the twelve tribes of Israel. And everyone who has left houses or brothers or sisters or father or mother or children or lands, for my name's sake, will receive a hundredfold and will inherit eternal life. But many who are first will be last, and the last first."

This passage is so misunderstood and misquoted and misused. I hope to help in a small way here. The disciples are incredulous at Jesus' teaching about the camel going through the eye of a needle and exclaim, "Who then can be saved?" You see, if you had a lot of money, then you were esteemed and thought to have a close relationship with God. Jesus challenges this assumption head-on. In fact, he says that a rich man cannot enter the kingdom of Heaven simply because he is wealthy. You can't buy your way into a relationship with God. It is impossible.

BUT…with God all things are possible. Jesus is placing the emphasis on the primary relationship that needs to be in place. God makes the impossible possible. In other words, the eternal life you and I are after cannot be purchased with coins or with accolades.

Whether we are aware of it or not, we often do things to enjoy the praise of others. "You're smart." "You're savvy." But if we slow down long enough and consider, this neither can be the riches we are after… the ones that last forever. For as soon as the person dies—mom, dad, brother, sister, co-worker, boss—their praise goes down to the grave with them. So these riches won't last either. You and I must press into the eternal life offered to us by developing and nurturing our relationship with God. Only then are riches put in their proper place.

But there's a nagging question I had as I began to consider these things. I alluded to it above. How did the disciples of Jesus' day begin to think that wealth was the indicator of a relationship with God? This, I believe, finds its roots in Father Abraham. And this really forms the foundational element for this book.

God wants to bless you SO THAT you will be a blessing to others. We saw it in Paul's teaching a moment ago, but we see it in technicolor in the very beginning of the Bible. In Genesis 12, God calls Abraham out of the land of Babylon saying, *"Go from your country and your kindred and your* *father's house to the land that I will show you. And I will make of you a great nation, and **I will bless you and make your name great, so that you will be a blessing**. I will bless those who bless you, and him who dishonors you I will curse, and in you all the families of the earth shall be blessed"* (Gen 12.1-3).

God does not shy away from telling Abraham that he is going to give him abundant wealth. The key piece, though, is the purpose. He doesn't simply bless Abraham with a lot of land and possessions to show how capable he is.

Unlike the plethora of prosperity preachers today who boast of their mansions and private jet(s), Abraham's primary calling was to distribute that wealth to others so that others would then know the power and might and grace of God. It is very clear, then, that God is not opposed to actual wealth. [*Note: I don't have time to go into a full-blown explanation of this here, but this truth is sprinkled throughout the Bible. Take, for example, the life of beleaguered Job. We often remember him with boils and undergoing great loss. But consider he had to have great riches to undergo such great loss...And don't forget that the epic ends with Job having those riches restored by God(!) twice as much.*]

But we need to bring this foundational chapter to a close with Jesus' teaching that informs the title of this book. In his infamous Sermon on the Mount, Jesus says, *"Do not lay up for yourselves treasures on earth, where moth and rust destroy and where thieves break in and steal, but lay up for yourselves treasures in heaven, where neither moth nor rust destroys and where thieves do not break in and steal. For where your treasure is, there your heart will be also"* (Matt 6.19-21). Couple this with a later teaching where Jesus says that the Kingdom of Heaven is *"like treasure hidden in a field, which a man found and covered up. Then in his joy he goes and sells all that he has and buys that field"* (Matt 13.44).

The key to the abundant and rich life you and I are after cannot be purchased with gold. You know that in your heart of hearts. We witness it every day in the latest celebrity news stories. Those who have no lack of material wealth are getting divorced again and going off the deep end emotionally and relationally and psychologically. We see it in the made-for-television reality shows where fighting persists and the empty darkness does not lift.

Let me level with you in utter transparency. I was scared to write this book. I was afraid of what people would think of me. As I mentioned, I have been in ministry for 25 years. I went to school with loads of pastors, missionaries, and ministry leaders. The misunderstanding of wealth is pervasive. So much so that people are afraid of making wealth because they are afraid of losing their souls. It's a good thing to be wary of. But that does not mean we ought to run from it. If the biblical witness I shared is accurate, and I know it is, then we ought to be first pursuant to God and happily receive whatever blessings he gives **so that** we can be a blessing to others. So that we can share that our treasure is not on earth where moth and rust destroy and thieves break in and steal. We can, then, point to a more lasting treasure…eternal life with God.

I was scared to say that getting and keeping wealth was not sinful or bad. In fact, when I told one friend the title of the book, he immediately cringed and squinted his eyes and said, "Now Matt, we don't want people to run after that." You see, that's the problem. Instead of slowing down and considering what Jesus actually said, we coddle our prejudices and run away from an opportunity to show the world a different way to be wealthy.

I want you to be rich. **So that** you can help others find true riches. I want you to live an abundant life so that you can share with those who lack. I want you to have many nice things that you can give up for the benefit of others.

When you are living out of your gifting by God, many people will be served. As the incomparable Zig Ziglar said, "You can have everything in life you want, [condition] if you will just help enough other people get what they want."

This book is an exercise in helping you re-discover how God has wired you. I firmly believe that God has made you in his image. And as his image bearer, you have the privilege and responsibility to engage the world with the unique combination of gifts that you have been given. The unique insight and interpretation of the world you have. As such, this is not an endeavor to simply increase your bank account. I am sure some of you picked this up to find out how you can add another 0 or comma to your paycheck.

I will be honest with you. This book does not promise you that outcome. BUT I believe that when you integrate your mind, body, and soul and align these three areas toward a common purpose in your life, your finances, your relationships, your emotions, your mindset, your health, and your soul will flourish and experience a truly abundant life.

Stick with me through this book. Do the exercises and learn how to improve and integrate every aspect of your life. If you move through this material slowly and deliberately, I know you will end up better than you started.

Now. Let's work on getting ultra clear on how to get and keep riches that will last!

It's Time to BE Better

I come across people all the time who look at their circumstances and wonder why they're in the same spot they were a decade ago. No motivation. No personal growth. No change.

Too often they look at the circumstances, rather than taking the time to consider why their circumstances are the same.

The short answer is that *your circumstances are directly tied to who you have decided to be*. Every word of that previous sentence is important. Read it again. Your circumstances are directly tied to who you have decided to be.

Let's take the answer in parts:

Your Circumstances.

The word "circumstance" comes from the Latin, which literally means "to stand" ("stance") and "around" ("circum"). In other words, the things in your life—relationships, job, savings account—all stand around something. They didn't just come to be *ex nihilo*. They were the direct result of *your actions* in the world.

You decided to ask that girl out. You decided to, well, have those kids. You decided to major in that subject and get that job. You said "yes" to certain propositions and "no" to other opportunities. You chose to save that money or invest that money or to spend that money. Your decisions.

I cannot tell you how many people blame others. They blame their circumstances as though they have no responsibility. There is a growing victim mentality in our culture. But this has always been the case. It may be more elevated or prominent now, but it's always been around.

"But Matt, I didn't fire me." Okay. Let's chat about that for a hot minute. Why did you lose that job? Perhaps you didn't perform like you should have. Perhaps you put off an air of arrogance. Perhaps you didn't build relationships with your co-workers so that they couldn't imagine the company without you. Perhaps you didn't turn in your report on time. Perhaps you were misaligned with the job and company in the first place.

You get the idea.

There is more of volition and action present than you might have given credit for.

Same goes for relationships.

"But Matt, he broke up with me." Okay. You want to go there? The fact that even bringing it up causes a bit of soreness tells you almost everything you need to know. Instead of understanding that life is about learning and growth, you put your hope, dreams, and identity in the other person. Perhaps your neediness of him pushed him away—a weight no person was meant to bear. Perhaps your inability to be yourself made him think he wasn't getting the real you—and he didn't want to settle for a polished, fabricated, and false you. Perhaps you were misaligned from the beginning and should have never said "yes" to him when he asked you out.

"But he cheated on me." Okay. Let's go down that hole too. First, he was wrong. He broke your trust. He was a weasel. That's on him. Honestly. It is best that you found out than continue to go down a path with a partner who was misaligned with who you want to be—an honest and loving person.

Are Directly Tied.

Did you notice that I used the word "misaligned" in both of those examples? That was on purpose.

As Sir Isaac Newton taught, "Every action has an equal and opposite reaction."

Now I don't want to get into the nuance that quantum physics brings into that observation. Suffice it to say the law is pertinent to the observable world…and holds true in the mental, physical, and spiritual spaces we inhabit.

You said "yes" or "no". You allowed things to come into your life and repelled others through your words.

Even in the case of someone forcing themselves on you (in the horrible cases of rape), they have to own their sin. You were a victim in that instance. But you have the decision now how you will let that affect you. It can either define who you are or you can assimilate that horrible action and become better.

Let me pick that scab just a bit.

You must hear this before I say this, though. The person who forced their will upon yours is to blame. It is his or her sin. It is his or her offense to be either prosecuted for and to make restitution for. That is not yours to own.

With that said, and this in no way implicates or puts you in the wrong or to blame. You could have been wearing a string bikini on the beach late at night alone when it happened. It's not your fault that he did that. That, my precious friend, is his fault.

You do need to own that you decided to be on a beach. Alone. At night. You let the relationship progress when you could have spoken up.

As multi-millionaire entrepreneur Tom Bilyeu says,

> *Extreme ownership is all about keeping your power. It hurts to admit that you're the only reason things aren't going well in your life. But if you get beyond the blame and shame game and into the action game, suddenly realizing it's all your fault is empowering. If it's your fault, you can make a change and get a different result. And there's nothing more powerful than that.*

Again. Hear this very clearly (especially on such a sensitive topic, but I wanted to use the most extreme example to make the point, and I am sure people will not hear me because the topic is too close to home or too emotive). You did not cause the person to sin against you. That. Is. Their. Fault. They were the coward. They were the uncontrolled. They were the manipulator. They were the wrongdoer.

Once you embrace that truth. It is liberating. Too often horrible people will say it's the violated one's fault because they shouldn't have been wearing that or in that place. It's not.

The magic happens, though, when you take back your power and take back your autonomy. As Bilyeu said, you can grow and learn from the horrible offense if you let it do its work. You can leave the manipulative environment. You can say "no" and tell someone. You can hit them in the groin and laugh at them. Even with what's already been done, I want you to put this book down and say out loud… "That's not my fault." Do it.

Now I want you to say out loud (if you're in a coffee shop reading this as I am in one typing this), "I am in control of what I do now." Please do it. For your own healing. For your own ability to move forward and take back your God-given power.

Let me share a story about a man named Joseph. He was an arrogant young man who thought he was better than his eleven other brothers. Yes. Eleven. He had good reason, too. His dad was not shy about letting those eleven know that Joseph was his favorite. He made him an elaborate coat that was bright and obvious. He made Joseph stand out.

One day Joseph shared a couple of dreams he had with his brothers that set them off. Essentially, they were going to bow down to him in homage. And not just them, but also their mom and dad. Put yourself in their shoes for a minute. You would probably roll your eyes. But then as you reflected on it, you probably would get pretty angry at such arrogance. So angry you'd like to put him out of your eyesight. And that's just what they did. They planned to kill him, but trafficked him to some Egyptian traders—not caring if they used him for sex or hard labor.

You can read more about this amazing story in the book of Genesis (chapters 37-50) in the Bible.

But to make the story short, Joseph was thrown in prison for two years on falsified charges by a woman that tried to rape him. He tried to maintain his integrity, but was punished.

Joseph is released through his trusted character while in prison and by taking advantage of an opportunity to counsel the Pharaoh. A door opened, and he walked through. He didn't hem-haw as to whether he should help a king who wrongfully put him in prison. No. With the opportunity he was presented with, he took full advantage because he refused to play the victim. In fact, I believe the crushing he endured by being trafficked and thrown in prison served to squeeze out his arrogance and to give him a perspective only someone who had gone through such pain could learn.

Joseph is re-united with his brothers. In fact, he provides food for them so they wouldn't starve. And when they repent for the evil they had done against him (notice, they own their sin!), Joseph is able to give a macro-narrative to that one scene in their life play. He said, "Don't be afraid. Am I in the place of God? 20 You intended to harm me, but God intended it for good to accomplish what is now being done, the saving of many lives. 21 So then, don't be afraid" (Genesis 50.19-20).

What a beautiful picture, not only of forgiveness, but how you and I can use the crap that is shoveled on us as fertilizer for growth.

That is your calling. To see your life as part of a larger narrative that doesn't end in your mire. But that God can use to bless and even save other people.

To Who You Have Decided to Be.

In Joseph's story, the entire narrative flips when he decides to be a certain kind of person. When an attractive and married woman propositions him to have sex, he says, "How then could I do such a wicked thing and sin against God?" (Genesis 39.9).

No one would have known. But he would. And he knew what kind of man he wanted to be. He wanted to maintain his integrity. He wanted to be a man of character. His brothers, who were responsible for him being in Egypt in the first place rather than enjoying the lap of luxury and more fine clothing, were wrong. The woman was wrong to proposition him. Her husband was wrong for wrongfully throwing him in prison. But he decided on his journey to Egypt in chains the kind of man he was going to be.

The operative words in the sentence we have been dissecting are "who" and "be". Notice the subtitle of this book again: It's time to *be* better. Life is more than what you have. What you have is a result of who you are. More specifically, who you have decided to be.

Don't let circumstances or other people decide for you. The truth is, they can't. The beautiful subplot of this grand story is that you decide who you want to be—regardless of other people and circumstances.

That truth provides freedom. That fact re-establishes the power you have in your own life, that you may not have been able to exercise for any of your life. But today you can begin to, as Rage Against the Machine so aptly said, "Take the power back."

In fact, I think it's appropriate to end this chapter with some selections from the song...and I'd encourage you to listen to it...So. Powerful! Of note, it will challenge our common sensibilities and give us the courage to ask whether we have grown complacent in our own lives. Have we largely spent much of our life coasting and assuming and presuming? Most people don't let other viewpoints in their lives because they aren't secure in their own views to let them be challenged.

In the right light, study becomes insight.
But the system that dissed us
Teaches us to read and right
So called facts are fraud.
They want us to allege and pledge
And bow down to their god.

Lost the culture, the culture lost.
Spun our minds and through time.
Ignorance has taken over.
Yo, we gotta take the power back!

The present curriculum
I put my fist in 'em.
Eurocentric every last one of 'em.
See right through the red, white, and blue disguise.
With lecture I puncture the structure of lies.

Installed in our minds and attempting
To hold us back.
We've got to take it back.
Holes in our spirit causin' tears and fears.
One-sided stories for years and years and years.

I'm inferior? Who's inferior?
Yeah, we need to check the interior
Of the system that cares about only one culture
And that is why
We gotta take the power back

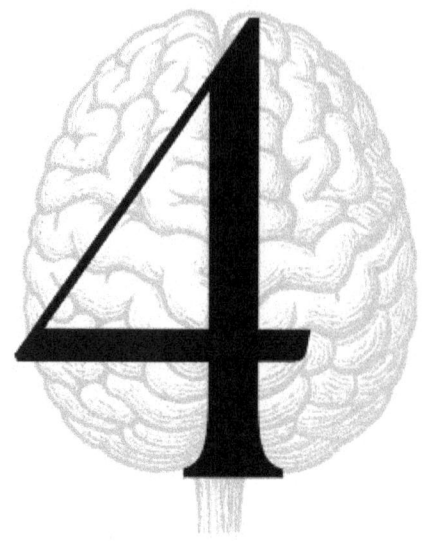

The Rich Mind

Carol Dweck broke ground with her work on what she termed a "growth mindset". This has been revolutionary to myself as well as so many others. I'd encourage you to watch her TedTalk if you want an abbreviated version of her seminal work by the same title. I'll summarize here.

In observing children who were given puzzles of varying difficulties, Dweck noticed that some kids would respond in despondency while others would exclaim, "Oh! Wow! I love a challenge!" The former she termed "fixed" in their mindset, while the latter she coined as having a "growth mindset"

What was it that made the difference?

Much of it was upbringing. Some of it was hard-wired. Sorry. No resolution to the Nature or Nurture debate. And that's actually good news. Why? Because you can take the power back. AND you can have a profound effect on succeeding generations in how you parent and mentor others.

Quite Simply: *What you do matters*. But more specifically for this chapter…What you *think* matters. What you think and believe drives your actions. We will get into this more in our chapter on the soul, but what you do demonstrates what you really believe to be true.

Both for yourself and for others. I look back on my life and it was both the positive examples that pulled me toward a greater calling. But being teased by others for my weight and strange accent (I moved from suburban Ohio to rural Kentucky when I was eight, which resulted in me sitting in my house watching television and eating white bread, literally!) pushed me *not to* be those kinds of people. What is more, by seeing what I did not want to be like propelled me to encourage and see the good in the unique gifting of others.

Future Growth.

The real amazing results of Dweck's study, though, came in following those same children over the course of their lives and seeing how they ended up.

And it makes sense, doesn't it? As Dweck said, a growth mindset embraces challenges, whereas a fixed mindset opts for blaming and giving up because "this isn't fair." As serial entrepreneur Ed Mylett says, the true breakthrough happens when we realize that life is not happening to you but for you. In other words, in embracing that there is a larger story you are a part of, you begin to realize that there is a Design. There is a plan. It's not up to you to figure it out—like finding a needle in a haystack, but figuring it out is directly tied to how you were created with particular passions and lenses to see the world.

If you get nothing else from this book, I want you to hear this loud and clear:

You were created for a beautiful purpose.

You are not a mistake. No matter how you came into this world...you were appointed to make a difference in this vast and intricately woven world.

It's when we let other people tell us who we should or shouldn't be that we lose touch with this God-appointed design for us.

Identity.

One of the key insights embedded in the research is the issue of identity...and it serves our purposes to pause for a moment and reflect on this.

Those with a fixed mindset would often be heard saying, "I'm so dumb." Or "I'm not good at puzzles."

The way this works out as we grow older is, "I'm dumb." Or "I'm not good at that." The secret sauce happens when we add a three-letter word. "I'm not good at that...yet." With time and effort, you can improve at anything.

We never look at a baby and say, "What's wrong with you? Why aren't you walking? It's been months of just lying around." Nor does a toddler give up on walking after it falls several times thinking, "I'm just not good at walking."

You have to extract the characteristic out of your identity.

Already / Not Yet.

One of the key teachings in theology is the in-between time you and I live in. In Christianity, this works out in the teaching that we *already* have eternal life, but we do *not yet* experience it.

This is a constant struggle with anyone trying to get better. We see where we want to be (not yet) and where we currently are (already). We know we want to make a million dollars a year or lose 20 pounds or be an exemplary father, but we see our shortcomings.

Let me encourage you with this, though. The sheer fact that you are envisioning those things in your life means that you're on your way.

Remember what I said in the last chapter that it's for lack of direction that people never get to experience the abundant life promised to them?

That lack of direction is endemic to our culture.

People are wrapped up in what others tell them they should or shouldn't be. They are preoccupied with entertainment. [Prime Example: How many people can rattle off statistics for their favorite sports teams, but complain that they're in a dead-end job?] People binge on Netflix while their marriages are crumbling under them. People are enslaved to pornography. And gossip—which says so much more about them not having anything of value talking about in their own lives!

You will do well to simply have this perpetual dynamic for all of us who want to be better than we currently are. You will want to embrace your humanity and your limitations. Those are good things to not only be aware of...but they provide the grace you need to actually move forward.

What happens when we look at life as a game that is never finished? We are constantly learning from mistakes and making adjustments in life.

Rocket Launch.

Did you know that the way a rocket gets to its destination is through mistakes?

We can often think that a rocket goes from Point A to Point B as though there is nothing in between. But that's not how it actually happens. Rather, there is a Point A and a Point B, but there are millions of data points on the way to the destination. In other words, there is Point A1, A2, A3, A4…

Let me explain. Once the rocket is launched, it pings back and forth (left and right) and is eventually guided to its destination. Think of that game Plink-o on the Price-Is-Right. If you're too young for that, imagine you're at the bowling alley. After hearing from too many people getting gutter balls (yeah, I didn't limit it to kids getting gutter balls, because adults need them too!) that they provide bumpers. As the ball is rolled down the alley, it bounces from bumper to bumper until it hits some pins.

This is a great encouragement for you and me. As John Maxwell says, we're either winning or learning. There is no losing unless you give up.

Atomic Habits.

Related to this is James Clear's bestseller called _Atomic Habits_. In his book, Clear says that we need to know who we want to be and create habits that will lead us there. He shares the image of someone breaking a large boulder. He is not going to be able to break the boulder in one hit. Instead, he has to make numerous, small hits in the same spot. The effect on the boulder is at the atom level. They are tiny, but no less important. Can you imagine the boulder breaker (is that what you call them!) waylaying on the boulder as hard as he could? He would quickly grow tired. He would probably hurt himself.

Instead, the power resides in the repetitive nature of his action. Not only the repetitive, but the precise nature. He's not just hitting it in a sustainable way. He's hitting it in the same spot over and over and over and over and over and over. Slowly…but surely…the boulder cracks. Just Google <u>"break a boulder" on YouTube</u> and you'll get the picture.

If you want even more multi-media encouragement, Clear has an excellent **8-minute video** on his website you can check out where he explains about getting 1% better every day.

This perspective is also called the Kaizen method. It has been described as "everyday improvement, everybody improvement, everywhere improvement." **Check this video out.** [For those not on an eReader, you can just Google search "kaizen".] It's really important for us to wrap our heads around this concept because true *and sustained* growth happens over time.

Perhaps you've been on a fad diet like I have. Trust me, I've tried *many*. While you can get results quickly, most times the weight comes back because the habit had not become interwoven into your identity. I do think that if you decide to make the change to lose the weight, it needs to be sustainable because you can actually do damage to your metabolism and organs with rambunctious changes to your lifestyle. Slow and sustainable is preferred. More on that in the next chapter.

Get S-M-A-R-T-E-R

As you consider how to improve, self-development expert, Michael Hyatt espouses what he calls **S-M-A-R-T-E-R goals**. He took his cues from the business world that talks about S-M-A-R-T goals and added a few tweaks. Instead of saying, " I want to lose weight." We need to be **Specific** and **Measurable**. I want to lose 20 pounds. What is even better is that your goals are **Actionable**. For example, " I want to lose 20 pounds" is good, but it's better if you say *how* (or what actions you will take to get there). I will lose 20 pounds by working out five days a week. And going deeper into this (and along with Specific) is saying, "I will lose 20 pounds by going to the gym 5 days a week for 1 hour doing 30 minutes of walking and 30 minutes doing 5 exercises for 3 sets of 10." Notice how granular I make it? A good test for goals is how many numbers you see in the mix.

Fourthly, Hyatt says the goal ought to be **Risky**. If you're 125 pounds, losing 20 pounds is probably not achievable (nor desirable...nor healthy!). I would add to this criterion that the goal should also be **Reasonable**. If you weigh 400 pounds, 20 pounds is easily attainable, but not Risky.

As he writes, "If you set goals that you know you can achieve, you aren't forcing yourself to rise to the challenge." That is, it doesn't inspire you to say, "I'm going to wake up by 11:00a everyday." It's not risky, not inspiring to set a bar so low that there's no challenge. You were created by God for growth. Just as our muscles only grow when they are stretched (and broken down), so also your growth will happen when you are stretched (and often broken down).

The fifth element to good goal setting is that your goal needs to be **Time Bound**. As one of my mentors shared with me, a goal without a date is merely a dream. To continue with our example, "I will lose 20 pounds by going to the gym 5 days a week for 1 hour doing 30 minutes of walking and 30 minutes doing 5 exercises for 3 sets of 10 for 90 days." My coach tells me that a reasonable and intentional amount of weight you can lose is 1-1.5 pounds a week if you are diligent. Remember, these elements all tie in together. In other words, your Time Bound element is tied to it being Risky and Reasonable. You don't want to try and do this in 30 days (not Reasonable) nor in 365 days (not Risky).

Hyatt then shares what he calls the element of **Exciting**. As another mentor of mine said, "If your why's don't make you cry, they're not strong enough." You want to link your goals with a reason that captures your heart. Why do you want to lose 20 pounds? To look good for the beach? To be healthier so you can live longer and play ball with your grandkids? You have to work diligently on capturing the why behind your goal, otherwise it will lose its power. A good goal not only captures your heart but it pulls you toward a future that compels you to be better.

The last quality of a good goal is that it is **Relevant**. That is, you need to take into account the stage of life you're in. If you just had your first baby, your goal should be to simply keep your newborn alive! Don't try and summit Everest or any elevation for a month…You are human and you have seasons that come and go. Self-awareness will be key to setting goals that matter.

So Good They Can't Ignore You.

So much of American culture is enmeshed in the narrative that you need to "pursue your passion". It is true, for many a salary is the price of selling your dreams. But dig a little deeper and you will find that even those who have pursued their dreams have found that there is a price to be paid of insecurity, boredom, fear, anxiety, and depression. Talk to any entrepreneur and even the most "successful" will share with you a laundry list of disappointments and discouragements. They will tell you of late nights and early mornings. Of betrayal and posturing of "friends". There is no magic pathway you are to take labeled "passion".

There's another path.

Taking the title of his book from comedian Steve Martin who said, "Be so good they can't ignore" when he was giving advice to a young comedian, Cal Newport believes that following your passion is a sure pathway to unnecessary pain. Newport doesn't believe we should despise our work. Rather, he writes:

> *Passion comes after you put in the hard work to become excellent at something valuable, not before. In other words, what you do for a living is much less important than how you do it.*

It's much like the concert violinist.

Not even world-renowned Joshua Bell picked up a violin and started playing. Rather, his mother gave him a pathway to sharpen his skills when she noticed him stretching rubber bands on a dresser to play music. Surely there are other children who have been just as inquisitive and creative. But harnessing that creativity was what set Bell on a path to be so good the world couldn't ignore him.

In an interview with him, there are two things we can learn.

First, quality of practice is just as important as quantity. When you put in the work to become better, you need to have a plan (more on that when we tie everything up at the end with some exercises to be so good the world can't ignore you either). It's one thing to practice your scales, so to speak. It's entirely different to pinpoint areas that need addressing and improving those.

I heard one successful entrepreneur say that we should simply double-down on our strengths and hire out our weaknesses. At one level that is true. At a truer-to-life level, you need to pursue well-roundedness.

Secondly, you need to be a well-rounded person. I used to be of the variety that said, "I'm just not a good listener." Imagine that! Most people aren't good listeners. You can't simply hire out someone to listen for you. What is deeper, and what we're going to focus on for the remainder of this chapter is becoming a high-quality person. Someone who is guided by character—not merely because it's the right thing to do, but deep down if you picked up this book, you're the kind of person that wants to be a high-quality person. More below. But hold tight. One other lesson to consider from that interview.

Bell says that even after 40 years of non-stop practicing, he still has to practice every day—especially when it's not convenient. He says,

> *I still need to practice a lot. You might think that after 40 years of practice you wouldn't need to practice anymore, but sadly it doesn't work that way. You still have to keep chugging away and perfecting. I hear that Tiger Woods still gets out on the driving range and hits balls for hours at a time. You'd think he'd know how to do it by now, but that's not how it works.*

Because we are always and ever will be works in progress, we will need to sharpen and address areas of lack in our competencies and character.

What you have swept out of your thinking is the idea that you will arrive at your destination. That, my friend, won't happen until your time on Earth is done.

Oh. One last lesson from that Bell interview—and this is a corrective to the hustle culture that dominates social media. He says, "It depends, but three to four hours, though there are days when I feel I can take a whole day off. You need to find time for the body to rest."

Did you hear that? Even from the greatest in his field, he rests. He doesn't worry that the next great virtuoso is on his heels. Rather, he tends to himself. And that can only come with a heaping dose of self-awareness (we'll discuss this in chapter 3).

Let's conclude this section on getting really good at a skill, and then you will be passionate about it. Are you ready for this atomic bomb of a concept? I wasn't, but here Newport writes it:

> *If you want to love what you do, abandon the passion mindset ("what can the world offer me?") and instead adopt the craftsman mindset ("what can I offer the world?")*

The problem with "hustle culture" and merely "following your passion" is that they start with the wrong question by putting *you* at the center of the world. That's a weight and a gravity you weren't intended to shoulder.

The question you need to begin with is *"What can I offer the world?"* The assumption before that question can be answered effectively is that you need to embrace the fact you were created with a purpose. A glorious purpose filled with adventure and wonder.

The world has a way of feeding off and fueling cynicism. When something good happens, people tend to say or think, "Oh, just wait. The other shoe is going to drop soon." Maybe. But what if the other shoe that is going to drop is part of a dance? A glorious dance where, like jazz or huddle offense that makes adjustments for big, game-changing plays, you see the adversity as part of the joy. That doesn't mean to say we should get excited about bad things happening. But it's the storms at sea that cause the rush of adrenaline…aren't they?

Virtue Ethics.

This section could be where your eyes start to glaze over because they aren't used to reading words that have been affiliated with prudishness and ivory towers. "Virtue" has, unfortunately, been given a bad name. People often think of self-righteous bugs that seek to look down their noses. "Ethics" is too often affiliated with tweed coats with patches on the elbows while the pontificator smokes a pipe—while he's a scoundrel at home.

That ought not to be the case.

Of late, there has been a beautiful and practical resurgence of what is called "virtue ethics". "Ethics" is simply how we live our lives. "Virtue" is simply the guiding principle of our ethics. For example, I can say "I just want to be a loving person." The next question should be, "What does it mean to be loving?"

It matters a great deal the goal or purpose for why we do what we do.

As you look across the span of human history, some of the greatest atrocities happened because of an ill-defined virtue. Either to feed a base desire for power or for a more refined understanding of a certain race taking priority over another, people have been tortured and killed while the perpetrators believed they were doing the right thing.

A less extreme example could be your desire for justice to be exacted in the world. Within the current political climate, both sides are screaming for justice. The justice of not having school shootings. Enmeshed within that good desire are a litany of sub-categories of justice that go into the calculus of the ethic or public policy of how we accomplish that worthy goal.

Consider for a moment, one extreme: there are folks who believe all personal guns should be banned. On the opposite end of the spectrum are those who believe that the more guns, the safer our society will be.

Who is right? What policy is most just?

Cardinal Virtues.

Discussion of a core set of virtues stretches as far back as Plato. Those core, or Cardinal, virtues are: Prudence, Justice, Fortitude, Temperance.

One of the greatest challenges I have had as an educator and pastor is the need to give people categories for their human experience. Specifically, the joy of counseling and coaching is helping people define their past, present, and future experiences. Much trauma persists in people's lives because they haven't been given a vocabulary with which to understand those experiences. Anxiety ensues because they are left with a flurry of emotions without the benefit of pulling those emotions into the light to observe them. More on how to do this in our chapter on spiritual formation and flourishing.

The most important question to ask and answer is: What kind of person do I want to be?

The Cardinal Virtues have proven to be a tried and true way to give contours and direction to this question.

Prudence.

Another way to speak about Prudence is to call it Wisdom or Good Judgment. It's unfortunate that people have written off the idea of prudence because of how ultra-religious folk have lived out the virtue. Ever heard someone being called a "prude"? When called this, the person is seeking to pejoratively say they don't know how to enjoy life or they are constricted.

Good judgment has been termed the mother of the other virtues. After all, if you lack good judgment, then you will not know what is just, courageous, or self-controlled at a given time in a given situation.

So how do we gain good judgment?

That is the question.

In our current relativistic climate, it can get you cancelled if you affirm that there is a right and a wrong. The ironic thing about this, though, is that every single person believes in a right and wrong. The problem is, they ascribe "right" and "wrong" to what they particularly think is right and wrong (relativism). This is not the place to go into a history of postmodernism and relativism. The point of this book is to get you to your New Rich Life. So we will not delve into deep philosophical discussions. Sorry. There are volumes you can go to for that.

You got this book because you are prone and pursuant to actual change in your life.

So how do you cultivate good judgment?

You have to be governed by an outside and objective authority. The word "authority" can often give people the heebie-jeebies. In its purest form, authority stems from the concept of "author". It is one who stands over and determines the rules of the game or the story that we are a part of. Shakespeare is the authority of his plays.

In a similar vein, the One who has created all things knows how they function and their *telos* (Greek for goal or end or purpose), their reason for being.

You may fall into the atheist belief system and think, "Not relevant." I want to ask you to, for the sake of argument, and for the greater sake of self-betterment, that you consider for a moment that there has to be some objective standard by which you live. At this point in your journey, you may simply subscribe to what is good for the hive is good for the bee. In other words, because we want to survive and thrive as a species, it is in our benefit to not kill each other. That is an objective standard outside of yourself. If you peel back the layer of social acceptability (or not acceptable in this instance), you will find that you have a personal revulsion to cutting someone's throat.

If you lived in Aztec or in the Ancient Near East, you would have to accept or make amends with killing someone to appease the gods. Even your own offspring.

See how letting society determine our values is not transcendent?

You may find yourself thinking, "Well, that's why we need to do away with the whole concept of gods and God." Yet, there are even more instances of atheistic societies who killed others for the sake of the greater good—according to whoever was leading at that time. General Mao, for example, determined that for the greater good of society, it was good to delete people from existence.

We need an authority to stand outside of our cultural moments and give us direction for how we are to live and move and have our being in it.

Perhaps your revulsion is rightly reasoned. You may have grown up in a church where the leaders skewed and used authority as a cloak for things that would get them power and help retain it. That is the point. They were not governed by an outside authority that stood in opposition to elevating a creature over others. They misused authority. Rather, the beauty of authority and its relationship to right judgment is a result of affirming that every human is made in the image of the Creator. As such, we each have inestimable value. Regardless of sexual orientation. Regardless of mistakes that have been made. Regardless of whatever has been done. Your value and worth is embedded in your being.

This is a great guiding principle as you consider *why* you were created. Rather than getting into the rightness or wrongness of particular actions (that's a necessary conversation for another time), it is vital that you have a guiding set of objective and outside principles that will judge your actions.

And in judging those actions, you are set on a course of better living.

Too often, the concept of judging has gotten a bad rap. Consider it in its purest form. When someone commits a crime, it is actually a very loving thing for both the society and the person to judge their actions as wrong. That begins the process of recovery. If you are doing something harmful to your body, it is right and good for me to judge your actions and tell you, "Stop putting that in your body." It would be unloving of me to let you continue on a path of self-destruction.

This entire discussion of Prudence has been necessary to simply get you to a place of submitting yourself to a higher law, an objective law that will be the criterion by which you measure yourself. In fact, let's use that word "measure" as a better option when we speak about judging. You see, a judgment is simply seeing a standard and measuring an act or disposition or person to that standard.

But the word "prudence" comes from the Latin word "prudens," which is a shortened version of the word "providens," which means "to see (videns) beforehand (pro-)". This is a great way of getting at the idea of prudence or wisdom.

When I consider many of the problems I've experienced in my decision-making in life—and the countless people I have counseled and coached, the most prominent feature of a bad decision is the failure to slow down and consider how this decision might affect me and loved ones long-term. To see ahead of time that saying this or doing that will result in a certain outcome. Granted, we are not God and we cannot bring to pass everything that we want with our thoughts and actions. BUT...insofar as we can think through the ramifications of a certain action, prudence gives us the ability to measure and move forward with a better decision.

One very easy way to add points to your prudence arsenal is to gather around you a group of trusted advisers. These would be people who share your same values and understand your tendencies toward certain behaviors.

Three cautions as you think through who would be in your counsel:

(1) Choose people that can be more objective. For example, you wouldn't want to ask your parents about a decision that would influence you moving away or moving toward them (because their counsel would be skewed to see you more either way you slice it).

(2) You must tell people in your counsel that you need them to be blunt, clear, and honest with you. By prefacing the counsel with that caveat, you will be more likely to get counsel you can use.

(3) This one might be the most important caveat. Most people say that they want counsel, but only want to gather around themselves people who will tell them what they want to hear. In my coaching program, the first set of questions I ask people contains this very probing one: "Do you really want to change?" Only you can answer this question. Instead of being quick to say, "Yes," I would encourage you to take a few

moments and consider your own history. Why did you get this book? When you have been confronted with unsavory truths in the past, were you quick to accept them or did you explain away the criticism? As famous philosopher and theologian Jonathan Edwards said,

> *Be advised to consider what others say of you and improve it to this end, to know whether you do not live in some way of sin...And though the imputation may seem to us to be very groundless and we think that they, in charging us so, are influenced by no good spirit; yet if we act prudently, we shall take so much notice of it as to make an occasion of examining ourselves ... it is most imprudent as well as most unchristian, to take it amiss, and resent it, when we are thus told of our faults: we should rather rejoice in it, that we are shown our spots ... we should improve what our enemies say of us. If they from an ill spirit reproach and revile us to our faces, we should consider it, so far as to reflect inward upon ourselves and inquire whether it not be so, as they charge us ... they are likely to fix on real faults, they are likely to fall upon us where we are weakest and most defective.*

In a very philosophical and verbose way, Edwards is simply saying, "Even in inaccurate criticism, we have something to learn." You can read the full exposition of this idea here or simply search for "The Necessity of Self-Examination" by him.

Or as Ralph Waldo Emerson said, "In my walks, every man I meet is my superior in some way, and in that I learn from him."

I find that I am a better person when I hold my hands open and receive what the world has to offer me. I have the opportunity to get better by listening. Even my "enemy" has a perspective that I could learn from. I may still disagree with some fundamental principles he has, but when have we ever been hurt by considering another perspective?

Prudence guides us to have counselors who will challenge our assumptions and limited perspectives.

One last example, I know a couple who have gone through some very difficult circumstances. They have run headlong into very ugly situations. Each time they have asked me for counsel, it was obvious that they had already made up their minds. If you bristle at me mentioning this, then you're not much different than most people. In fact, this couple is not much different than anybody. You see, we can mull things over and over in our minds and then come up with a solution and we go to people to double-check that we're not crazy. The problem, though, is your counselors should have been welcomed *into* the process and not after the fact. You are putting your counselors in a very precarious situation. After years of counseling, I have resolved never to give advice to someone if they use the phrase "God told me to…" It has *never* ended well. They despise me for telling them something contrary and despise me even more if it turns out I was right. That's why the question of whether you really want to change is of paramount importance. Most people give lip service to change and wonder why they don't. It's due to being mentally convinced but not volitionally convinced. That is, they know in their minds they need to change but their hearts are not drawn to a better reality.

Temperance.

Unfortunately, this word got a bad rap in the 1920s with the temperance movement when "prudes" forced legislation that made alcohol illegal— the Temperance Movement. Whenever you try to force a conviction as a law, it will not go well. As a result. A proliferation of alcohol and rule-breaking ensued.

Of note, I believe the Temperance Movement actually incited people to break even more laws. That is, once someone says, "That's a dumb law," it's not too disconnected for them to deduce that *all* laws are baseless and matters of conviction that they don't need to follow.

Take, for example, when someone who grew up in an ultra-religious environment that taught it was wrong to go to the movie theatre. Once the person goes to the theatre, it's not too long for that person to see that freedom has been kept from them, and they run headlong to a slurry of other "illegal" activity.

The virtue of temperance, however, is much more integrated than a simple set of rules.

As Jocko Willink has famously written, "**_Discipline Equals Freedom_**".

The point about discipline is that it puts boundaries on our lives for a temporary pleasure for a longer-lasting pleasure. Temperance, in this way, is actually a liberating virtue and not a purely constricting one.

Consider my marriage to my amazing wife. I am bound to her by the cords of love, but I am also cordoned off from experiencing love from other women. The growing polyamorous movement in the United States has lost sight of the glory, beauty, and power of exclusive love and rights to the heart of another. There is a lot of posturing and philosophizing of how their love is more expansive, but it misses the power of monogamy. Side note: Many in the polyamorous movement have tried to have the glory of exclusive commitment in what they term hierarchies, while they have subordinate relationships. Of course, there is a lot of nuance and a lot of explanations folks would offer to justify opening their marriages.

I believe that they are closing themselves off to the power of exclusive love and personal development.

Take another example of what the Temperance Movement did get right. Many in our culture find delight in getting drunk at clubs and with friends. They are pulled to the beauty of letting go of inhibitions, but the next morning is a testament to the problem inherent in not having boundaries. Wine is a gift from God. It ought to be treated as any other gift, with care and as it was intended by the giver.

All this to say, guardrails are good for a dangerous road for life to flourish. Boundaries are good for a garden for plants to flourish. The discipline of working through conflict and to receive love from one person is vital for relationships to flourish.

As humans, we inherently don't like boundaries. This has been the issue since Creation. The story of Adam and Eve is appropriate here.

Unfortunately, the story has lost its power for many due to familiarity. I would argue that our culture is largely unfamiliar with the story; otherwise, there wouldn't be the tendency to indict God for being petty because our first parents ate a piece of fruit. That's like saying we shouldn't be angry with Benedict Arnold for uttering a sentence. It was over-the-top for the world to get angry with Judas for simply greeting Jesus with a kiss on the cheek in the Garden. {Check out these other salacious betrayals.}

The issue is not the act as much as the motive for the act. Just like Adam and Eve doubted God's character and right to rule his Creation. They doubted his goodness. So also we doubt the goodness of boundaries. So we set up a variety of our rules stemming from our own desire for self-rule. The problem with this pathway, though, is the same problem we saw earlier with Prudence...

When we come up against another self-ruling person, who is diametrically opposed to my self-rule, survival of the fittest must be the arbiter of what is true and right. We need an objective standard outside, and that stands over all the little, autonomous self-governing beings. Rules are good because they enable true human flourishing. The problem stems from people coercing others to abide by their convictions, which have become rules for them. Rules are good when they are seen as a means to an end and not the end in themselves. This, I believe, is where the Temperance Movement (and any other movement that pushes a conviction as a coercive agenda) went astray. It is good to not get drunk—not least of which are the health problems of a fatty liver that result from years of abuse—because of the almost immediate effect it has on vomiting and being out of your right mind. That alone should be enough to tell us that it is not good for us to over-consume alcohol.

The same is true for over-eating, though. The same is true of over-sleeping or over-working or over...you get the point. Contrary to popular belief, too much of anything is eventually not good for you.

Justice.

There has been a lot of talk of justice recently. And rightly so. Justice is a beautiful and good pursuit. The issue of primary concern is how we define justice. Better. What is the telos or goal or aim of the justice we seek?

Much of the issue that caused the 2020 riots all over the United States stemmed from the need for systemic reforms in the justice system—specifically, the need for accountability and transparency in law enforcement. As people initially took to the streets to peaceably protest against the heinous acts of injustice, the protests quickly became the platform for opportunistic political maneuvering and outright riots. Many were left scratching their heads as they saw people scream out for justice as they unjustly broke into and stole private property in the name of justice.

True justice is when humans are treated humanely. True justice takes place when the stewarding of the Earth takes priority in our use of its resources. True justice happens when law is meted out appropriately so that true human flourishing can happen.

Similar to the issue of temperance, it is vital to have clear guidance on how we ought to conduct ourselves and promote the good of others—Earth, plants, animals.

The word justice actually stems from the Latin word "iustitia," which has the connotation of rightness. On your word processor, you can "left justify" or "right justify" your text. This simply puts all the words of the margin on that pathway.

Are you seeing a pattern?

The fact is that justice has an edge to it. Whereas temperance and fortitude (coming up next) have a hemming in and a direction set out, respectively, justice guides the disposition or the rightness of what is owed to others (see Thomas Aquinas for a fuller treatment of this and

Josef Pieper's wonderful work called *The Four Cardinal Virtues*). The magisterial theologian and philosopher, Augustine of Hippo, wrote, "Justice is a habit, whereby a man renders to one his due with constant and perpetual will" (*City of God*). If something is due to someone, the question must be asked, "Why is there anything due to another person?" In the West, due to our inheritance of Christendom, we largely assume that humans have rights. But why? Why not see people as hindrances to my advance? Why consider my neighbor as equal in value to me?

Even asking these questions probably gives you uneasiness. That feeling stems from the largely assumed value of other people. But where did this value come from? If we are simply products of evolution, we cannot be an end in ourselves. Rather, we are stepping stones to a greater evolution of the human race, and those who stand in the way of human progress and betterment are better off done away with.

You see. We largely assume the value that is inherent to human beings. But without understanding that every human being has value, regardless of sexual orientation or the number of chromosomes they have, justice is simply arbitrary. At least true justice.

Therefore, as with the previous two virtues we have looked at, it is vital to start with the foundation of God. That is, God being the one who imbues men and women with inherent value. As the Bible says, men and women have been created in the image and likeness of God.

Fortitude.

I remember as a young boy watching The Ultimate Warrior wrestle in the WWF (now WWE). He was a physical specimen. He was strange to listen to. But he was life-changing to watch him wrestle. He was an atomic bomb contained in a human body. He would run around the ring at breakneck speed and hit his opponents. But like any good wrestler, he had his challenges with others and would find himself beat up and on the verge of collapse. Of note, I remember watching him lay on the ground spent from blows he had received and the sheer amount of energy he spent himself. As he lay on the ground, almost motionless, the announcer said over and over again, "Does he have the intestinal fortitude to go on?" It was another way of saying, "Does he have the guts? The strength? The resolve?"

I love the adjective he used in front of "fortitude". The strength to carry on has to come from a place deep down inside of you. It's not something anybody can convince you of. You have to feel it in your bones.

In the Hebrew Scriptures, the word for heart is actually the word for "guts". The word in Greek gets at the innermost part of who we are *splangizomai*. You can almost feel it coming up from within you when you say it out loud.

We have spoken of justice being a direction of the rights-ness of an action. Fortitude speaks to the inner motivation to move toward the right. Without a clear and firm resolve, it doesn't matter how beautiful and worthy the goal is if we are not convinced in our heart of hearts—our guts, the innermost parts of who we are—we are not going to move in the direction that we need to.

Fortitude is also related to the word "force" or "strength". If you remember from physics, force = mass x velocity. Force, therefore, is the product of a body and how quickly it is moving. A feather doesn't provide nearly as much force as a bowling ball. A bowling ball rolled by a five-year-old will not have as much force as one rolled by a 25-year-old. As this relates to our discussion, you cannot expect to have the strength to stand against the travails of life if you have not invested in your mass. Better. You must invest in the presence you bring to the world to exhibit and provide force for movement of stationary objects in the world. Additionally, you need to take responsibility for how quickly you move through the world. Now I'm not suggesting that velocity is sheer speed. It is focused energy in a certain direction. When you chop down a tree, hitting the tree in the same spot with the same amount of strength will have better results than hitting the tree in different places with the same strength. Get it?

There is a need for people in our world to have focused energy. For people to be people of weightiness and substance.

There are too many people who are not fully present in the world around them. There are others who run around in a frenzy in a hurry of activity, but have very little effect in the world around them because they are simply bouncing off the walls. I would submit that these latter folks are simply reacting to the world around them rather than bringing their presence into the world.

What do I mean?

Fortitude assumes you have a presence. A form of being that you bring to the world that influences it in such a way that if you were not present, the world would continue as it was. God created you to bring force into the world by presence and movement. Many of us have forgotten that we were created to effect change in the world. It doesn't have to be so cataclysmic as Martin Luther King, Jr. or Abraham Lincoln. But we must always remember, these men, while imbued with great courage and fortitude, effected change because of the numerous supporters that brought their presence and energy into the world. The countless marchers and soldiers who laid down their lives for a greater purpose.

We remember a few names of the myriad of people who exhibited great fortitude to effect change. They brought their presence and energy to move the chess pieces of history. On the other side of this story are even more people who sat idly by and did not do anything about the hate and murder done day after day. As long as it didn't come knocking on their doors and the status quo was not disrupted, they did not want to say anything.

The Primary Question.

You have heard the quote from Hamlet, "To be or not to be," that is the question. The question beyond that question is "To be what?" You see, while existence is a good thing, sheer existence is not the goal of your life. Merely existing is not a worthy existence. You were created with a grand purpose and with a great design. No matter how much popular culture would have you believe that you are a product of happenstance and a lottery, you know deep in your soul that there is more to life than random relationships. We don't live like that because we intuitively know there is purpose and design in the world.

"Choose your own story" may look great on an Instagram post but only makes sense in the context of a greater story. Even the resolute nihilist lives and seeks to find meaning and purpose in his life, even though his worldview has no foundation for it other than utter subjectivity. The nihilist can never say that something is right or wrong. The honest nihilist can only say, "That's wrong for me."

This is so intellectually dissatisfying because we know that abusing others is wrong. Killing others is wrong. But if I am the arbiter of what's right and wrong for me, I can never tell you what you ought or ought not to do, try as I may.

In his excellent, very practical, and very probing book, _The Character Gap_, Christian Miller honestly writes, "Our hearts are not morally pure, but they are not morally corrupt either. Rather, they are a messy blend of good and evil." This is helpful as we seek to be better people because we have to embrace the fact that we have both honorable characteristics and self-centered qualities. This helps us own our shortcomings so we can actually get better. The first step for a sick person to make is to admit she is sick. That doesn't have to be condemnation, but it actually provides relief. You see, in our heart of hearts, we know something is askew in how we relate to the world. There is a gap in our character of who we want to be and who we are.

In an interview with Dr. Miller for the My New Rich Life program, he made it very clear that the way forward is to identify what character qualities you want to have. That is, how do you want to be remembered? This translated to what I call the **"Deathbed Exercise."** Some coaches have people write their eulogies. I think that can be helpful. The problem is we have trouble imagining what people will say while we are dead. I believe there can be power in considering you being on your deathbed and overhearing what is being said of you in real-time by those you love and have given your life for.

Perhaps you could put this book down now and consider this question: What qualities will those sitting around your deathbed call to memory as they consider your life?

I venture to say it wasn't as much the accomplishments you made as much as the kind of person you were: hard-working, resolute, kind, tender, gracious, loving, etc. When your time to die comes, you really don't want to be remembered for making millions of dollars, as much as you want to be remembered for what you did with those millions of dollars. What kind of reparative work in the world did you have a part in? How did you use your money to help others? They may call to mind your trip to Spain as a family. But it's the memories made while on that trip that will last.

So it is, as we close this chapter, you need to spend some serious time reckoning with: *"What kind of person do you want to be?"*

By way of application, use the next two blank pages to write down what you overhear on your deathbed.

Deathbed Exercise

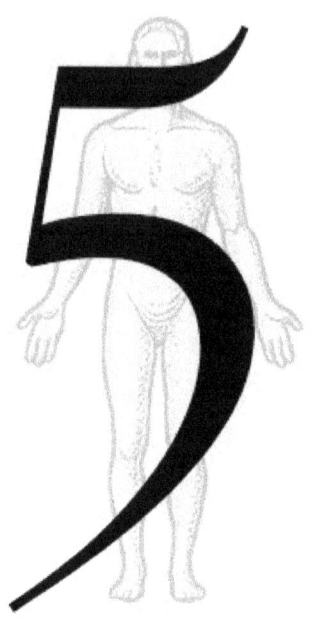

The Rich Body

I grew up in a home and culture that didn't prioritize physical fitness. It was fine to be on a sports team, but it was primarily for the social element and not the focus and pain and growth that would ensue. My family prioritized the life of the mind. Getting good grades and a good education were vital to living the good life. I am eternally grateful for this emphasis.

Yet, as in all things in life, there needs to be balance. And in some cases, for a season, we need to swing the pendulum in the other direction. After all, isn't that what brings life to the clock? It moves from one direction to another and produces friction and movement. This isn't to imply that we are frenetic and move from thing to thing just to produce friction in our lives. That's chaos.

Rather, we need to see where there is an underemphasis in our lives and readjust. We constantly readjust because life constantly changes. I have seen this in my life in vivid ways. I will focus on my spiritual life, but my relationships or health get neglected. And so on. Day by day, we need to adjust our lives to align with our values. We will do this in very practical ways in the final chapter of this book. For now, let's spend time considering our physical health and the need to prioritize it.

Proper Balance.

I still remember the Food Pyramid that came in vogue while I was in elementary school. It was a visual representation of what a balanced diet looks like.

The problem with this pyramid, though, is that it depends on what your commitments are. In other words, there is no one way to balance out your diet. In other words, you need to know and understand how your body responds to various foods.

I am sensitive to dairy and gluten, for example. If I followed the Food Pyramid from the 1980s, I would probably have some serious gastrointestinal issues. In fact, I did. I loved to drink milk and thought it did a body good. I would drink skim milk (ew!) right out of the carton (without my mom looking). I remember many times throughout my growing up that I would be doubled over in abdominal pain. But I never asked the question, "What did I eat that made me feel like this?" No. I thought it was a fluke. I never went through the necessary step of thinking through the relationship of what I ate and how I felt. I realize now how crazy this sounds. I mean, I knew that eating a whole pizza or two bowls of ice cream would make me feel lethargic and gross. But those were the extremes. The necessary step was to be micro-attuned to my body so that I could easily consider: "I feel bloated. What were my last two meals?" OR "I've got a lot of gas." OR "I feel energized." The necessary step is asking, "What did I do soon before this feeling?"

Let's Practice. How do you feel right now? Do you feel energetic? Sluggish? Bloated? Sore? Strong? Achy?

Now: Where do you feel those sensations? Ankles? Stomach? Lower Back?

For example, I feel tired and achy. No, really. As I write this in a coffee shop, my eyes are heavy, my mind is wandering, my middle back muscles are sore. Before this revelation of a tight connection between feeling and food and habit, I would have simply chalked up today as a hard day. Most high-achievers are wired this way. We are so task-oriented that we are largely unaware of our surroundings or our insides. We are so busy thinking about the next thing on our to-do list that we don't slow down long enough to simply be aware of how we are feeling —not merely emotionally (we'll discuss that in the next chapter!), but physically how our muscles and guts and bones feel.

Here's an exercise to practice self-awareness in our body. Go through your five senses and describe what you are experiencing. I'll go first.

I **hear** the instrumental beats playlist coming through my AirPods right now. I feel a throbbing sensation from having them in for the last two hours.

There. I took them out. That feels better! Now I hear the people at the table across from me. Oh, and that table too. And the music playing over the speakers.

I **see** the people talking. The ladies in front of me are having a heart-to-heart. The three girls at the next table are laughing and are lighthearted. The person next to me has her headphones on and is not to be bothered. Hm. There are a lot of ladies at this coffee shop. In fact, I just counted. 70/30 ratio right now. I begin to notice the decor of the coffee shop. Very Pottery Barn-ish. No wonder.

I **feel** my fingertips on the keyboard, and they are a bit chilly. My butt hurts a bit from sitting for the last three hours working on this book and a talk I will be giving this weekend. My eyes are heavy because I woke up at 1:00 a.m. and couldn't go back to sleep until 3:00 a.m.— Nightmare woke me up! My back is sore. That's an easy reason; I did a slew of kettlebell swings and burpees yesterday. I need to talk to John at the gym on Monday to find out if that's where I should be feeling pain there or not. Nah. I'll just Google it. "Is middle back pain normal after kettlebell swings?" There you go. It's due to poor form! I'll need to correct that by straightening my shoulders, engaging my core (I feel NO pain in my core…that's probably because I didn't engage it!), and not rounding my back. I will implement it next time.

I **taste** the aftertaste of the coffee I am sipping, and the tip of my tongue is raw from nervously fiddling with the back of my teeth. I'm hungry! No breakfast, and it's getting to be lunchtime.

I **smell** the roasted coffee…and my coffee breath.

Okay. You get the picture. The key here is to practice micro-cognition of what is happening in your body. Be specific. It is vital that you attune to your body. Especially as you begin to modify and take your diet and exercise seriously, it will be key to adjust and stay motivated. You adjust when things are out of alignment—i.e., bloating and unusual soreness (see middle back pain from kettlebell swings!). You stay motivated as your body feels less lethargic and bloated and tighter as muscles you haven't engaged before begin to activate.

Food.

What is your favorite thing to eat? No, really. After a long day at work, when you get home and go to the pantry, what do you reach for?

My vice was chips and salsa. When I started to take corn out of my diet, due to its inflammatory nature, I changed to trail mix. It's a healthier choice for sure.

Perhaps you need to consider what you mindlessly eat (more on that in a minute). Evaluate whether your go-to food is inflammatory, high in calories, promotes healthy recovery for your body, etc. What is it? Does it need to change? My next step is to move from trail mix to carrots, celery, or apples. Why? Because trail mix is high in calories and I LOVE the flavor…so I eat more than one handful unless I think about it.

Mindfulness has been my problem. I'm going to share a tool my coach shared with me (that I modified)…in fact, it's in My New Rich Life Workbook, so you may have already seen it. If you haven't got the Free Workbook, head over to www.MyNewRichLife.com and get a copy for free.

The tool is a **7-day Food Journal**. I actually just called my coach this morning elated because I have dropped several pounds just this week. Granted, a lot of the weight was from water retention. But even that is a victory! My body shouldn't be retaining that much water.

What I shared with Dan "Kill Mode" Long this morning was that I didn't realize how mindlessly I eat. You see, I grew up in a home that if you felt hunger pangs, you just popped some chips in your mouth and took care of it.

Having to journal about every single thing that goes in my mouth has made me slow down before I take a second handful of trail mix (from a Tootsie Roll to peppermints, yes, I'm serious! Keep track of every single thing).

This may not be your problem, but I venture to bet that if you are driven, like I think you are, you spend very little time slowing down to consider what you're putting in your body. If you do, kudos! But for the rest of us mindless eaters, we need to be told to slow down when we eat. Along with the 7-Day Food Journal, try these exercises:

Count when you chew. Count one-one-thousand, two-one-thousand from the moment the food hits your mouth to the moment you swallow. How long does it take for one bite? Try to increase the amount of time. For me, it's currently moving from four seconds to six seconds.

Take smaller bites. I have a huge mouth. I used to do the dumb trick where I could fit my fist in my mouth. Yes, I could do that. Fortunately, I don't know if I can do that or not.

Suffice it to say, I take LARGE bites.

My wife gently reminds me to not only slow down (see previous paragraph), but to take smaller bites. If you're prone to put a mound on your fork, consider putting a hill. Consider filling half your fork. Just because you have a big mouth doesn't mean you need to fill it.

Get a smaller plate. Studies have shown that you eat less when you have smaller plates. It looks like more food, and you're less likely to go back for seconds.

In fact, resolve now (I had to!)...do not get second helpings. Ever. I don't care how good the food is.

This is a BIG problem for me. I don't eat low-quality food; I eat a LOT of high-quality food. I don't remember the last time I had a soft drink or McDonald's (probably twenty years). I remember I had to learn this—and am still learning it.

Just because I eat healthy food, that does not mean I can eat more of it. Just because I'm diligent to eat Keto, doesn't justify putting three handfuls of trail mix in my mouth (which I did last week!), that's over 400 calories right there. Or, that's 40 minutes of walking to put it in perspective.

Drink a gallon of water. Seriously. Try to drink 1/2 gallon by 1:00 p.m. and the other 1/2 gallon by 6:00 p.m. Learn from my failure here. I have to be cognizant to divvy it up like this, or I end up drinking 3/4 gallon around bedtime…and that drastically affects your sleep (so key to a healthy life!).

Here's your life-changing **7-Day Food Journal**.

Remember.

Write <u>every</u> <u>single</u> <u>thing</u> you eat. It's not fancy, but if you do it, I promise the discipline will change your life.

DAY	FOOD	CALORIES
MONDAY		
TUESDAY		
WEDNESDAY		
THURSDAY		

DAY	FOOD	CALORIES
FRIDAY		
SATURDAY		
SUNDAY		
NOTES:		

Definitely not rocket science. The key, though, as in all things in life, is actually taking the action and doing it. I actually put mine on a Google Sheet so I have it with me wherever I go. Makes it easier to record in real time what I've eaten. Like budgeting tools, I have found if I don't write it down immediately, I forget to and I lose interest because I get overwhelmed with trying to go through my day (or the last two for that matter) and putting it down in the journal...so, I don't. Of course, you might be more disciplined than me!

Supplements.

I go through a lot of details regarding supplements. Even if you eat as clean as possible ("clean" meaning organic, unprocessed food), there are vitamins and minerals you cannot get only from food. I know there will be folks who disagree with this, but the majority of nutritionists agree with this. Until convinced otherwise, I will go with them.

So if you buy my argument (or lack of it, ha!), let me suggest some key vitamins and minerals you need to supplement in your diet. When possible, you need to take these in liquid form for better absorption and efficiency. By all means, if you're going to take in pill form, take in capsules and not the pressed-together hard pills (aka, tablets).

These:

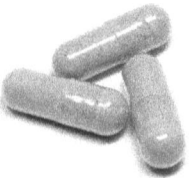

Not These:

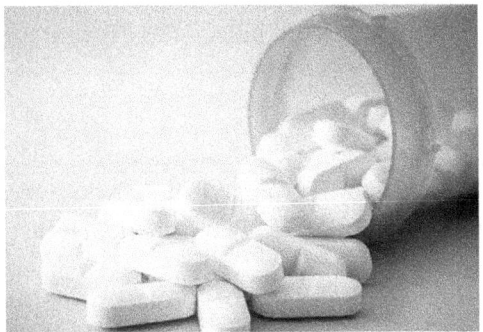

The vitamins you want to take (I share a more comprehensive list in My New Rich Life Program):

D3+K2
Immune system function. Bone growth and density. Health of many tissues in the body, including prostate, colon, and breast. Cardiovascular health.

Irish Sea Moss
Boosts the immune system. Supports healthy digestion. Promotes thyroid function. Aids in weight management.

Berberine
Blood sugar control. Weight Management. Cardiovascular health.

Zinc
Metabolism help. Immune system support.

Protein Shakes

A healthy diet consists of a lot of protein. You will find that you feel fuller longer. Unless you go for a carnivore diet, you will not get the requisite protein. A good rule of thumb is to eat your weight in grams of protein.

Fermented Fish Oils

Vitamins A and D. Helps with inflammation. Bone health. Joint pain. Eye health. Cardiovascular health. Better mood. Healing of the stomach and gut.

This is by no means an exhaustive list. I share more in My New Rich Life Program.

If you haven't joined yet, please go to www.MyNewRichLife.com and sign up!

If you want to go further down the rabbit hole, I highly recommend you look at Shawn Wells' extensive research and writing on supplements. Other good health gurus to follow are: Shawn Stevenson, Daniel Amen, Gary Brecka, and Layne Norton.

Simple.

There has been so much written in health that you can get overwhelmed. Trust me. I know the pain. My wife has joked with me that I have tried every fad diet under the sun. My weight has, by far, been my greatest challenge. I grew up in a family that didn't prioritize their health. The life of the mind was paramount. While I am so grateful for this emphasis, I wish I would have made disciplined decisions regarding food and exercise earlier. This has been a recent journey over the past 15 years. I am no expert, but I have been a guinea pig. From hard caloric restriction (with MediFast) to speed pills cloaked as fat-burning pills to Keto to extended fasts...I have tried a LOT.

One thing I have become convinced of, though, in the past two years is this: Pick a sustainable plan and stick with it. Sure. You may need to make some drastic changes immediately—like going through your pantry and throwing out all processed sugars. Go ahead. Do it now!

But to lose the weight and to keep it off, you need to choose to change your lifestyle.

That's what My New Rich Life is all about. Changing who you are...then what you do will flow from that.

One simple way to do this immediately is to also change the way you talk. Instead of saying, "I can't eat sugar." Change that sentence to "I don't eat processed sugars." Notice the difference? One is a rule from the outside. The other is a disposition that is rooted in who you are. It is a fruit of your volition. No one or no diet is making you do or not do something.

Another note on sustainability. While I shared the 7-Day Food Journal, that is not sustainable. It is a tool, however, that will help you develop an awareness of how you eat and what you eat. After a week or two of tracking everything, you will find that you are more mindful of what you put in your body.

Once you get your mind engaged in what your body is doing, though, you need to begin implementing rhythms of eating the kinds of foods you are eating. In other words, simply by being mindful you will be less likely to eat foods and piling on the calories. If you're going Keto, go Keto. Don't get bogged down in the micro-details of peeing on a keto strip to make sure you're in ketosis (yep, I've done that too!).

You can definitely dial your nutrition in. At this point, however, you simply want to be mindful and disciplined in following your plan.

Extended Fasting.

The discipline of fasting has gained a lot of traction over the last decade. I won't bore you with the studies. You can...Google it (ha!). Instead, I want to share a few insights I have had with my brief foray into disciplined fasting (the last three years).

First of all, I encourage you to go on an extended fast in the next month. That means, try fasting 48 hours. A quick hack is to eat at 6:00 p.m. You will begin fasting immediately at that point. You are utilizing your sleeping hours to get through the pain of fasting. That is why breakfast is called break-fast after all! Over a period of 48 hours, 16 will be while you sleep.

A second hack is to make black coffee your friend. The caffeine will help you have energy and suppress your appetite. If you don't like black coffee, learn! If you insist on being belligerent, then try tea. Not sweet tea (I'm in the southern United States, remember). Hot tea or unsweetened tea is your friend. Stay away from artificial sweeteners. Stay away from honey. Just don't do the sugar thing!

Side note: You will find as you go through a detoxing from processed sugars, you will crave them less. Trust me. Apples, bananas, and grapes will taste sweeter. Our current processed food world is so pumped full of sugar, we don't even realize how desensitized we are to the sugars in our food. I said this was simple...not easy. Just draw a line in the sand, bright lines as Tom Bilyeu calls them, to say, "I will not eat candy." I know that could be hard. Try it for a month and tell me you don't feel better. I dare you.

A third hack when it comes to fasting—specifically, sustained fasts—is to have naturally flavored water by your side at all times. When I say "naturally," I mean I put lemon or apple cider vinegar in my water to give it flavor and for their added health benefits. Some people also put cucumbers in their water for a refreshing and cleansing result. Either way, stay away from those crazy water flavorings that tout themselves as vitamins (I'm looking at you, Mio flavoring!). They aren't necessary and will simply prolong the time it takes to re-train your palate. After all, that's a subsidiary benefit of what I'm encouraging you to do.

Intermittent Fasting.

Something I have been religiously practicing over the past two years is what is called "intermittent fasting." Sounds fancy. For me, though, it's as simple as not eating past 7:00 p.m. and not eating again until 11:00 a.m. (16 hours). I promise you, my stomach gets pangs around 10:00 a.m. sometimes. Not all the time. You get used to the feeling...and frankly, I kinda like it—not in a masochistic kind of way, but in a confidence and an "I have self-control" kind of way.

Cognitively, you are able to focus better. Scientifically, the energy your body would be putting toward digesting food in the morning is available for cognition. I am writing this at 1:30 p.m. right now in a fasted state, and my neurons of ideas and connections are firing faster than I can type!

As you're getting started, I would recommend doing intermittent fasting with a friend. Preferably someone you see throughout the morning, with whom you would be embarrassed to eat the scone in front of if you're both committed to fasting. As you get more disciplined, you will rely less on accountability, and it will be your normal way of being.

I'm not interested in debating people who say you better eat breakfast. That's fine if you want to eat breakfast. No judgment here. I am simply sharing what I have seen, studied, and practiced for several years and have seen the benefits in substantial ways. The only way you will know if it's right for you is to try it for a few months and see how you feel.

Everyone is wired differently, and there is no one-size-fits-all in diet. The best thing you can do is practice different ways of eating. I would recommend trying intermittent fasting for a couple of weeks and sprinkling in an extended fast at least once in the next month. Yes, it will be painful, but journal how you feel notwithstanding the hunger pangs. Note your energy levels and cognitive abilities.

I would also recommend removing gluten and dairy from your diet. Perhaps both at the same time to see quicker results. One at a time if you want to scale it back. You may find you have a gluten or dairy sensitivity and you didn't even realize it. That's how it was for me!

A couple of diets you can try on for size, in addition to the Ketogenic diet, are the Whole 30 diet, Paleo, or Carnivore diets. The key here is to be mindful. To be disciplined. To be consistent. To be sustainable.

One last thing before I get into Fitness in the next section. You need to be willing to believe that our culture is not a friend to your health and lasting happiness. You need to be willing to trash the popular and follow the crowd. This is a typical mantra in our culture, but few actually delve into the implications. I just got done watching a popular television talk show where the guest just made a sandwich by squeezing cheese onto bread as "easy cheese" sandwiches. Well. It's easy enough to make that kind of sandwich, but I wouldn't be patting myself on the back that you actually did something noteworthy. You may have saved yourself some time, but you just subtracted time off your life span—not to mention the quality of life just processing that muck! Take the time to just read the Nutrition Information on a can of "Easy Cheese" and this is what you find: 80 calories for 2 tablespoons. Total Fat: 6g; Cholesterol: 10mg; Sodium: 430mg; Protein: 4g. That doesn't sound that bad…BUT she probably put on 8 tablespoons, so that's 320 calories. Add the two slices of white bread: 134 calories (67 each); Fat: 2g; Carbs: 26g; Protein: 4g. So you have an Easy Cheese sandwich of 454 calories. You're not going to just eat that. But say you did, what you need to be even more concerned about is the vicious processing that food goes through and what the raw materials are of that food. Just look at the ingredients from the Easy Cheese! Whey, Canola Oil, Milk Protein Concentrate, and Cheddar Cheese. Cheese isn't even the first ingredient in a cheese product. Don't even get me started on the preservatives and extras! There is nothing easy in Easy Cheese when it comes to your genuine health.

You have to be willing to be governed by a different set of values when it comes to your health.

Oh. And now the chef just made peanut butter hamburgers?!

The key to any diet is for you to slow down and consider what you are putting in your body. Too often we succumb to our cultural need for speed and efficiency and never pause to consider that "easy" isn't good.

Fitness.

We complicate things with the smorgasbord of options for how we get the six-pack abs or boulder shoulders or junk in the trunk. Just like we considered the character qualities we want to exhibit, we also need to consider what we want out of our bodies. As my friend and bio-hacker extraordinaire Ben Greenfield aptly says, we are souls with a body. What is key to understand is that our bodies dramatically influence our spiritual lives (and vice versa). Too often people prioritize one over the other. A better understanding to hold is that what I do with my body largely determines the direction of my soul. The discipline I value in my soul will affect how I view food and the discipline and rigor I am willing to submit myself to.

The key, just like with your choice of diet, goes to simply making a choice and sticking with it.

Something, though, that you may not have considered is that your physical fitness can be an act of spiritual growth. As you sweat. As you strain. I want you to consider that you are training your body and soul for discipline. When moments of temptation to do something that compromises your integrity, you will have known the strain of exertion. That is, to be the kind of person you want to be, you have to learn delayed gratification. Physical exertion practically teaches you how to do that.

So do this. Pick a plan that you can sustain and stick with it.

When I go to the gym, I am astounded with the exercises people put them through. I get it. People read a guru on the benefits of hanging upside down and doing arm extensions to provide greater oxygenation to the brain and extremities, yada yada. The problem, though, is that, like a diet, that is simply not sustainable...

I have had five different fitness coaches, and let me share with you the common thread with all of them: Choose simplicity. Simplicity encourages and empowers consistency. That really is the key to sustained fitness.

I would encourage you to set a standard of how many days a week you want to work out. How long? And select the same exercises for each of those days. Do this for six months. Don't change your workout regimen. Don't chase a promise of big gains or big losses.

For example, I have set a standard of going to the gym 5 days a week. If I get to go more (and I do), that is simply added discipline. I went to the gym this morning and simply walked on the treadmill at a brisk pace for 40 minutes and stretched. I went to the sauna for 20 minutes and took my morning cold shower. I will go back this afternoon to walk and push weights. Today is Monday, so I know I will be doing the same chest and back exercises I have been doing for a looooong time. One of my fitness coaches said he had done the same routine for twenty years—and he was an accomplished bodybuilder.

One of the added benefits of doing the same exercise is that you don't have to keep trying new exercises. Yes. You can sprinkle in some fine-tuning exercises. Instead of simply doing chest arm flies on a machine, you could go to the cables and provide some variations on the form to hit different smaller muscles (setting the cables lower or higher).

Another benefit of doing the same routine over and over again to train yourself to appreciate the mundane. We too often get enamored with novelty. Not only in fitness but in relationships. We find our eyes straying to a different person than one we are in a committed relationship with and imagine being with them. By training ourselves to be content with the mundane in the gym, we are training our hearts and eyes for the mundane in other spheres. And the beauty of this contentment is that you can go deeper and cultivate more meaningful depth to relationships. Further, on the issue of fitness, you can grow to see actual progress in your strength. If you start a new exercise every week, you have to start at square one. If you do the same bench press, you can actually see your strength increase because you have built on the foundation of the movement.

I am going to share my spreadsheet I use to track my exercises so you can set up your own—or use mine! Notice that you have your exercise and weights right there and could even put this information in a graph to see the progression. Confession: I have not done that…but I could!

	Exercise	Week of...	Week of...
MONDAY	Bench		
	Arm Flies		
	Push Ups		
	Upright Row		
TUESDAY	Leg Press		
	Leg Extension		
	Calf Raises		
	Back Extension		
WEDNESDAY	Preacher Curl		
	Shoulder Flies		
	Barbel Curl		
	Pull Up (Bicep)		
THURSDAY	Lat Pull-down		
	Sit Ups		
	Burpees		
	Bent Over Row		
FRIDAY	Bench		
	Shoulder Press		
	Incline Bench		
	Arm Flies		

Exercises.

Within my program called *My New Rich Life*, there is another workout formulated for my coaching group by another coach of mine, Dan "Kill Mode" Long. If you would like that regimen, please join our growing tribe of high-achievers who want to better themselves in mind, body, and soul. There's a QR code in the back of the book you can scan to get a special discount.

Something that I will give you that's in the program is a morning routine I follow and would encourage you to as well. It is a series of simple stretches that will get blood circulated and stretch your ligaments and tendons to get ready for the day ahead. We will get into that at the end of the book, but it is very important that you have a morning and evening routine you follow religiously. I would encourage you to make this **5-minute stretching routine** part of those.

Sleep.

One last element that you need to consider when it comes to your fitness is sleep. There has been a growing catalog of studies as to the benefits of deep sleep. Here are some keys to good sleep I would encourage you to consider:

Darkness. Instead of having a nightlight, darkness encourages deep, regenerative sleep. This means even the little red lights that are on any electronics in your room should be blacked out (a little electrical tape can help with this).

Phones. Our cellphones emit waves that we would do well to not have around us while we sleep. My wife and I put our phones on airplane mode. My phone is not on my bedside table. I used to have it there for when I got ideas that popped into my head—as they inevitably do as I relax. Rather, I have gone analog with my notes for the evening. I keep a little scout notepad so I quickly jot something down and then go back to sleep.

Blue light. Along with cell phones, televisions emit a blue light that disrupts good-quality sleep. If you are going to watch television in bed, you can either wear some blue light-blocking glasses or make sure you have about an hour of time between watching television and turning your lights out.

Weighted Blanket. This has been something Ashley and I have been using for a couple of years now, and it is a game changer for good sleep. Get one!

Same Times. Our bodies thrive on routines. Aim to have your wind-down time and waking-up time the same every day. Yes. Even the weekends. Too many times people get into a good rhythm during the week but mess it up Friday and Saturday nights so that their body's natural rhythm is shot because you stayed up too late. In these cases, it can take up until Wednesday when you're back on your normal schedule. I aim to have my lights out by 10 p.m. every night and wake up by 5 a.m. every morning. No exceptions.

Buffering.

One of the benefits in learning to listen to and be in tune with your body is knowing when you need to step out of your routine to recuperate. I remember one of my mentors saying that he would rest when he got sick. I do not affirm that way of grinding down your body and its immune system. Instead, you need to learn how your body is responding to the world around you. For example, just last month I spent the month not having my alarm set and simply waking when my body felt rested. Instead of pushing myself to get up at my normal 5a wake up time, I forced myself to stay in bed. Why? I could tell that my sinuses and respiratory system was not in top shape as pollen and dust and other allergens were being swept into the spring air. So…I spent the last month letting my body rest. On top of that, my youngest child had (up to that point) been crawling into bed with us around 2 a.m. and intermittently kicking me and elbowing me and waking me up throughout the night. Instead of pushing ahead like I normally would, I had learned to listen to my body and extend grace to my routine so that I let my body heal from low-quality sleep and an immune-wracking environment.

There are numerous studies on the need for sleep to help in stress relief, anxiety, depression, and weight loss. I have a list of such books in the Resources section of My New Rich Life. Check them out.

Cold Showers.

You've probably heard a lot about this crazy phenomenon. In hearing it, you might have reacted like me, "Let's do it!" Or you might have responded by, "Nah. That's a little too intense and crazy for me."

I was probably on board immediately because I trusted the sources that told me about it. And as I delved more into this discipline, I realized either I was crazy or too proud to at least try it. When myriads of health experts and very successful entrepreneurs swear by it, we do well to perk up.

It is true, there are tons of health benefits related to cold showers (cold plunges are even better…sticking your face in ice-cold water also has benefits if you are on the cheap or unable to do either the plunge or the shower). The main reason I enjoy taking cold showers is due to the mental strength it produces. I don't get up excited to jump in a cold shower. In fact, I recoil and try to think of fifty different ways why it's stupid. What happens every time I let the cold water pierce my skin is a piercing of my comfort and sloth. I am skewering my tendency toward letting my emotions determine my choices.

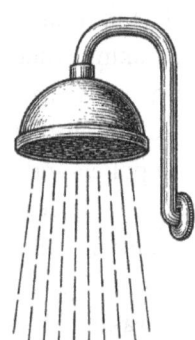

If you need more convincing, just Google search it, and let the experts convince you.

As we close out this chapter, I want to end simply by underlining the fact that our physical bodies have a dramatic influence on our spiritual lives. Our emotional lives. Our relationships. Our minds. If you feel down in the dumps, go for a walk! If you just got broken up with, drink a quart of… water! If you feel sore all over, consider what you've been eating and experiment. Don't give into the popular notion that you're just getting old. Look on any Instagram account and you will find 80-year-olds doing pull-ups.

For too much of my life, I prioritized the mental and spiritual life over the physical. I heard Paul's admonition, "Physical training is of some value, but godliness has value for all things, holding promise for both the present life and the life to come" (1 Tim 4.8). I had emphasized the "but" in this passage and didn't consider the truth that physical training has value. Certainly, we need to keep it in its place. Having a six-pack can become an idol just as much as praying to the gods and wanting rain for the crops.

I have gone through bouts of depression throughout my life. Not clinical. But definitely dark spirals of doubt and lethargy, and seeing everything as not worth it. Stuck in a rut of comfort, I didn't see that pushing myself into discomfort and sweating would pay dividends in my spiritual life. Whether I realize it or not, when I do difficult things with my body, I am training my soul for when difficult things happen in life. When I lose something precious to me. When someone doesn't return affection. When my job doesn't go the way I'd like it to go. These difficulties will happen in life. By willingly putting myself through pain and strain, I get my soul ready for these challenges. When I feel lactic acid build up in my legs after leg day or my lower back being a little stiff because of bad form, I learn to adjust my form and accept the painful growth that must happen as a result of putting forth effort to change.

What a beautiful picture of what our lives are intended to look like. In the next chapter, we are going to consider our inner life, and I hope you see the tight connection between your outer and inner life.

To end this chapter, I'd like you to use the next two blank pages to simply write your honest evaluation of where you are in your physical health. I think simply writing things down enables us to see reality. Answer these questions: Am I happy with my physical health? If not, how would I like to improve (weight loss, strength, flexibility)? How is my eating? Should I cut some foods out that aren't serving my larger purpose of vibrancy and longevity? Write out your plan for the next week. What exercise will you introduce? What foods will you replace? And with what will you replace them? If weight loss and gain has been a struggle for you, spend the rest of the time simply reflecting on Why has it been a struggle. What habits do you have in eating and exercise?

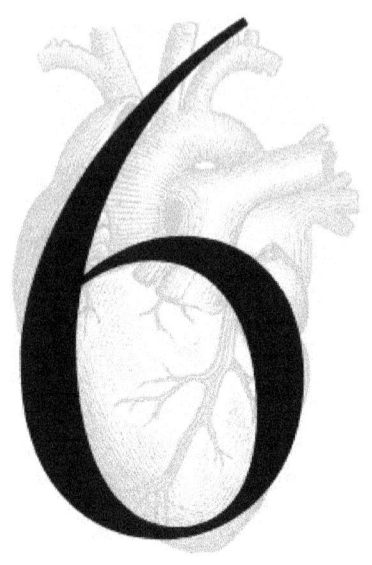

The Rich Soul

One of the key differentiators between what I am offering you, compared to other personal growth folks out there, is an emphasis on the need to strengthen your spiritual life. I love personal growth. If I were in a bookstore, I naturally gravitate toward this section of the store.

Many Christians can either be very quick to accept all that the personal growth gurus are selling, or they are highly skeptical. I find somewhere between skepticism and full adoption is a good place to be. Because I am a Christian, the Bible is my final authority in belief and practice. That means that everything I learn needs to be run through the sieve of whether it is in line with God's Word or contradicts it. That doesn't mean, however, that the Bible is the only thing we need to read. It provides everything we need for life and godliness, for sure. But there are so many things, practically speaking, that can nuance and help me apply those truths even more.

For example, when I am going through self-doubt or fear or anxiety, many people of faith would chalk it up to my need to read the Bible more or pray more. But what if I am already praying and reading my Bible every day?

You see, this was the quandary I found myself in when I had bouts of darkness in college. Well-meaning people would ask if there's some secret sin I was harboring or what lesson God was trying to teach me. They would tell me to read my Bible more and pray more and fast more. These I did, but the darkness didn't lift.

So what is a person to do?

While this isn't a book about getting out of depression, I can't get into all the tactics I've used to get out of my funks in life. For the purposes of this book, let me just say that the tactics that I have found helpful did not come from the Bible. So, as a person of faith, should I put them aside and just read more psalms?

Trick question. It's a both-and. It's a good idea to both read the psalms and to scour practical ways from professional coaches and counselors to get out of the funk.

After all, isn't that why you got this book? You wanted practical ways to enrich your mind, body, and soul. You wanted to be stirred up in love and good works. You wanted to be encouraged through practical means toward your self-improvement.

The motivation behind writing this book and starting My New Rich Life was due to seeing a hole in the personal growth space. I would watch, listen, and read person after person give very practical strategies for how to schedule my time and implement a workout routine.

But the gaping hole came when some coaches would talk about the importance of our soul and spiritual life and leave it at just deep breathing and meditation.

I've been counseling and coaching people for over two decades in how to develop their spiritual lives. I've done it across countries and cultures. I've seen that so many people want to develop their souls, but they haven't had trustworthy or trained guides in this area. So…they are left with deep breathing and meditation, but never told what to meditate to. And if they are given that information, it too often stays in the area of affirmations that may or may not be true. To simply say, "I am rich. I am worthy. The world is for me," doesn't really fill the longing in each of our hearts.

Now, don't worry. I'm not going to start proselytizing you…or giving you the "Jesus Juke"—where I'm talking about one thing and then, all of a sudden, I try to convince you to become a Christian.

While I am a Christian and believe that Jesus is God's answer to our greatest need, I want people of other faiths and no-faiths to be able to read this book and learn how to develop themselves spiritually in very practical ways. If you would like to talk about how Jesus changed my life and view of the world, I would be happy to do that anytime!

For the purposes of this book, I want to give you some tried and true practical wisdom from centuries of spiritual experts. And when I say experts, I don't mean simply theories. I mean the real-deal folks who went to the desert and developed their inner life through blood, sweat, and tears…literally.

Born in the Desert.

One of the greatest helps to me in my spiritual life was my introduction to those known as the desert fathers and mothers. Attributed to Saint Anthony, who went out to the desert to wrestle with his own demons, the Desert Fathers and Mothers followed Jesus' paradigm of going out to the desert (see the Gospel of Matthew, chapter 4).

Throughout the Bible, the desert has been the place where God deals with his people. He revealed himself to Moses after he had left a life of luxury in Pharaoh's palace. He purified and showed himself faithful to Israel to bring them through the desert, where their feet did not swell and they never went hungry. He preserved his people in the wilderness of Exile in Babylon. And Jesus, following in this great paradigm, went out to the desert to be tempted by the devil and to prove his worth and to not succumb to temptation like Adam and Eve did. The desert is the place of desolation. But it is the place of re-birth, if we will let it do its work.

When we embark on this journey of being reborn and re-shaped, we must begin from the inside. No amount of discipline. No amount of goal-setting means anything unless you have first cultivated your heart and soul.

Sometimes you must actively pursue going out to the desert. Our world is full of comfort and distraction, which keep you from developing an interior life that is formidable. So many of the problems we see in our culture—particularly with anxiety and depression—stem from the neglect of the heart. Many people, especially religious people, mistake religious activity with an abundant spiritual life. They could not be more mistaken.

It was the religious leaders of Jesus' day that he excoriated and called to repentance. So many houses of worship are filled with blind guides who tell people that their breakthrough is coming. The job they want is on the way. Their bank account is getting ready to overflow. They have mistaken the abundant life Jesus promised to his followers with a cheap imitation wrapped in dollar bills. The rich life is one that attends to the interior life and doesn't mistake shiny objects for true gold.

Other times you will be forced into the desert. As I write this, I just found out that my father passed away last night. It was entirely unexpected, and he struggled for ten days in the hospital to regain his health and strength. I have wept for so many days as I have grieved losing the man who provided surety, strength, and love. And then regained hope that he might pull through. And then lost it again. My heart feels numb in this moment. My soul feels very dry.

Many of you reading this are going through your own desert. What difficulty or doubt are you being forced to stare at? Don't busy yourself with distraction. Sit in the desert. Sit in the pain. The pain and suffering have been allowed by God into your life to mold you and shape you into the person he created you to be.

Tony Robbins has recently opened up about the abusive environment in which he grew up. He has said, the moment of strength happened when he looked back on his life, grieved it, and realized that without those painful moments, he would never be able to be the man he is today. Of note, he is now able to help others who have been hurt in a similar way. He has transformed his gall into a balm for others.

So it is in your life. Do not mistake this as justifying offenses against you. As I said in the beginning of this book, that is their sin to confess and own. But the major question you have to answer and reckon with is, "What will you do with that pain?" Will you let it do its regenerative work, or will you let it eat away at the edges of your soul? Will you let it harden your heart so that you protect yourself?

I have often taken the pain of being left behind by friends or the embarrassment of being the butt of people's jokes…I've often taken that pain and put an armor on. I have shared just enough to appear vulnerable, but always held a little back so I wouldn't feel the brunt of abandonment or not being enough. But this is not what God intends for us. We were created with hearts that feel pain because we have loved.

CS Lewis wrote about the pain and vulnerability of love in *The Four Loves*:

> *To love at all is to be vulnerable. Love anything and your heart will be wrung and possibly broken. If you want to make sure of keeping it intact, you must give it to*

no one, not even an animal. Wrap it carefully round with hobbies and little luxuries; avoid all entanglements. Lock it up safe in the casket or coffin of your selfishness. But in that casket, safe, dark, motionless, airless, it will change. It will not be broken; it will become unbreakable, impenetrable, irredeemable. To love is to be vulnerable.

A Tale of Two Kings.

I want to share a story of two kings in ancient Israel. There was a good-looking, tall, strong young man named Saul who was chosen by Israel to be their first king. He had all the kingly attributes you would look for. There were, however, things that bubbled up that were brewing in his own heart.

First, he was hiding when he was called out. Instead of instilling confidence in his soul, he doubted whether he should lead God's people. This is not to say that a king is to have bravado or a big ego. But if the prescribed means of anointing a king are present, that king should take confidence from the process and the choice.

Second, this lack of confidence shows up throughout his life as he struggled with fear of losing what was his. Instead of embracing his calling and fulfilling it through study and obedience to God's words, he dabbled with other methods of securing control.

This leads to a *third* problem in his heart. He put confidence in religious actions rather than the one to whom these actions pointed. Specifically, the point at which God took the kingdom away from Saul happened when Saul became impatient because he was fearful that he would lose a battle. In an effort to manipulate God, he offered a sacrifice in haste rather than waiting for the prescribed means through a priest.

The second king whom God chose to replace Saul was a modest, humble, seemingly insignificant runt named David. When David was being selected, there is a significant phrase that God tells Samuel the priest: "Do not look on his appearance or on the height of his stature, because I have rejected him. For the Lord sees not as man sees: man looks on the outward appearance, but the Lord looks on the heart" (1Sam 16.7).

This is the key indicator of a deep and lasting and royal lineage—a heart that is resolute. In another place, Proverbs tells us, "Keep your heart with all vigilance, for from it flow the springs of life" (Prov 4.23).

Our world is fascinated with the exterior and neglects the harder heart work that's necessary for truly lasting change.

It is from the heart that physical change begins to happen. When I began to learn self-control, that translated to not overeating. When I began to learn the beauty of discipline, of doing the mundane, I began to feel the aches in my joints go away.

So it is with our spiritual lives. It might have been years since you've considered the need to tend to your soul. You have neglected a deep cultivation of your interior life. If this is the case, you will find there will be aches and pains. You will find first, though, that you need to overcome the inertia that has probably set into your pursuit of such work.

I cannot tell you how many times people tell me that they want to pray more or journal more or fast more or…Just like working out physically, you need to stop overthinking it and compromising on choosing the path of least resistance. Just like muscles grow by being torn down, so also your spiritual life is built up through constant tearing and repairing.

This chapter we will consider various spiritual disciplines that are tried and true…and have been for centuries. You and I do well when we learn from those who have gone before and tilled the rocks and soil to find a way to foster deep growth and vitality.

Spiritual Formation.

Before we get there, I want to introduce you to a phrase. "Spiritual Formation" is the practice shaping our interior life. The imagery is likened to a potter's relationship to the clay. When I lived in Argentina, I took a pottery class to further understand this phenomenon—and to have a bit of a hobby to relieve stress!

As you consider a potter and clay relationship, you have to first consider that there needs to be intention. The potter looks at a lump of clay and determines beforehand what he will create. You also need to consider what you are wanting to be true of your spiritual life. What are the virtues (that we discussed earlier) that you want to cultivate?

One way to get to the answer is by asking yourself, "What is one thing I would like to change in my life?" You could start with what are called the theological virtues of Faith, Hope, or Love. Do you find yourself fearful when it comes to life? Do you find yourself constantly downcast and unable to see the light? Do you find yourself given to criticism as your default response rather than warmth and encouragement for others?

You could then move into what are known as the Fruit of the Spirit: Love, Joy, Peace, Patience, Kindness, Goodness, Faithfulness, Gentleness, and Self-Control. Get your eyesight laser-focused on one of these and first ask God to cultivate these in your life. After all, they are called a fruit of the Spirit, which implies the result of the Spirit of God working in your soul.

No matter how hard you try, you cannot muster these fruit into being. God works these into your soul…but you must first ask.

God, unlike how many perceive him, is not stingy. He is not reluctant to give you good things. He delights to do your good and for you to enjoy the world and life he has for you.

So you've got your intention. What's next?

Perfectly Imperfect.

Before you embark on this shaping that needs to happen in your soul, you have to embrace that the process is the point. For most of my life, I have unwittingly subscribed to the lie of perfectionism. I, growing up, found that if I succeeded and did really well in school, then I earned people's applause. So, I calculated, if I achieve more, I will be loved even more.

The key that has opened the door to a deeper and abiding soul change grew from seeds of acceptance. That is, God loves us so much that he loves us as we are. And he loves us so much that he doesn't let us stay where we are. That is, we are in a constant state of change. We are either tending to the matters of the heart or neglecting them.

As a father, I love my children tremendously. There's not a thing I wouldn't do for them. This started from the moment I knew Ashley was pregnant with each of them. This love for them started the moment of their conception. What did they do to earn that love and willingness to fight for their good? Not a thing. In fact, they simply needed. They needed nourishment and diaper changing and shelter and affection. They did not start cooking me meals or shining my shoes. They simply existed. So it is with our Heavenly Father. He loves us as his children.

But I would be a poor father, indeed, if I didn't help my children mature and grow into the best version of themselves. Does my love waver for them based upon whether they mature? Not at all. Yet, as their father, I would neglect to truly love them if I didn't teach them how to go to the bathroom on their own or how to make their own lunch or how to pick up their rooms and make their beds. True love is transformative.

We are on a journey of self-actualization. Of becoming the kind of individual God created us to be. We each have unique gifts and expressions he has put us in the world to share with others. But the beauty and the power of real self-actualization happens when we come to a deeper understanding of who God is. As we meditate on and reflect on his character of love and justice, we are transformed. The Apostle

Paul wrote that as we behold who God is, we undergo a metamorphosis into his image. We begin to reflect this benevolent and beautiful Being in our actions and dispositions.

This is what Jesus was talking about when he admonished us to be perfect as our Heavenly Father is perfect. It is a picture of completeness or wholeness that happens when we meditate on the Perfect Being's power and strength exercises on our behalf. That is empowering, indeed.

Arrival at some plane of existence of perfection. It is the joy, excitement, challenge, and growth that happens in the process of approaching that perfection. That is the joy and wonder of being alive. Realizing that we constantly change in light of his unchangeableness.

So how do we get to that path of change and growth?

Differentiation.

Differentiation is a term used by counselors to affirm the need to identify the world we inhabit and distinguish ourselves from it. We each come from a particular family in a particular geography at a particular time. Something that is very key is learning to differentiate who you are from these surroundings. Very few people do this hard work because it...well...works. And it can produce a bit of anxiety too. When we begin to identify patterns and behaviors we grew up with that we don't want to be true of us, it can be painful. In a sense, we can feel like a betrayal. We can feel that we are forgetting where we came from or, better, fearing that those we grew up with will think that. Whenever someone tries to do something different or become someone different, those that knew you and were comfortable with who you were will begin to be uncomfortable as they are forced to reckon with their own life choices.

I cannot stress this enough when it comes to spiritual formation. You must identify what you did not like in your childhood and what you appreciated. Even more nuanced. To appreciate things from your upbringing but deciding not to bring those things in because they do not shape you into the kind of person you want to be.

For example, I grew up in a home that prioritized the life of the mind. Studying hard and getting good grades was the priority in my life. Note, this was not due to some external pressure from my parents. Rather, it was my interpretation of how I could receive love and recognition from my parents and others. One of the beauties of differentiation is being able to identify this distinction. Immature people assume their interpretations are accurate.

Perhaps you interpreted your parents in a certain way. So you began to mold yourself into perceived expectations.

I had to decide not to bring that interpretation of my upbringing into my parenting. Rather, I chose to bring balance in academics, physical fitness, and spiritual formation. This felt like I was judging my upbringing. And in some ways, it is a judgment that that was not best. This will continue to be the case and struggle for you as you decide who to marry (to the chagrin of parents), how you will raise your kids (education, health, and discipline choices), what career you will pursue, and so forth. Again. You must identify and differentiate what kind of person you want to be from the person you have assumed you were supposed to be.

But you might be reading this and thinking, "No, Matt, my parents really did tell me that if I didn't bring home all A's, they would be disappointed in me because I embarrassed them." To that I say, That is horrible. I am sorry you had to experience such merit-based love. The power, though, resides in being able to see such a bad example of love and saying, "I am thankful that I learned to push myself beyond what I thought I was capable of. I am thankful that I did well in school because it paved a certain life and lifestyle I now enjoy. BUT. I do not want to bring such merit-based affection into my home." You were given a certain environment to grow up in so that you could bring a certain perspective…and a differentiated perspective into your new world and the generations in your family that follow. You don't have to simply adopt that way of being in the world. You can and must set about that hard work.

I want you to put this into practice. So I want you to write this down. It's preferable that you get a journal (more on that below), but for the sake of expediency, I want you to do the following exercise. If you're like me, though, you're tempted to just keep reading. Fight that urge. After all, you picked this book up because you wanted a change. In order to experience that change, you must do the work. So slow down and take a few minutes. It will be the first steps on deep spiritual formation. Answer the following prompts:

My family would be characterized by the following adjectives (shoot for at least five adjectives):

I am thankful for the following things I learned when I was a child (think 8-12):

I am thankful for the following things I learned when I was a teenager (13-19):

If I could change three things about my upbringing, it would definitely be (note: this step might be very hard for you. You are not betraying anyone. You're not condemning anyone. You're not forsaking anyone. You are identifying unhelpful and unhealthy character qualities in your family of origin and setting about correcting them):

My earliest memory is:

This memory was sweet/bitter because:

If I could change one thing about my growing up, it would be:

Silence & solitude.

What you've just begun is a journey of self-discovery. Because you did the work so few do in their lives of considering where they have started on their journey, you at least know your coordinates. You will begin to see why you get angry when your kids don't pick up their rooms. You'll be gin to see why you don't pick up your room. Why you are skeptical and cynical and doubtful and fearful and sure of yourself and…

One of the things I prided myself on growing up was that I was sure of myself. But, even in the midst of that confidence, there was a nagging sense that people would find out that I was faking it. I was constantly critiquing myself.

For two years of my life, I thought about killing myself pretty much every other day. I wondered if anyone cared if I was around. How many people would be at my funeral? Would there be anyone at my funeral? Would they think I was a coward for giving up? Did what I did in the world matter at all?

These are the questions that went through my mind constantly. In my bedroom. At night. In the quiet. Left with my thoughts and free of distractions and the watching eyes, I was able to wrestle with who I really was.

Throughout the day, I was a good conversationalist and I made people laugh.

But in the silence, I was left with my thoughts. As philosopher Blaise Pascal said, "The eternal silence of these infinite spaces terrifies me." This terror was not unique to Pascal. Much of the human condition is riddled with self-doubt and self-loathing…but we busy ourselves with noise so we don't have to listen to what our inner self is screaming to us.

Psychotherapist Karen R. Koenig says, "People often fear being alone because they are uncomfortable with their thoughts, which race and upset them. They like being out with others or keeping busy because interaction and activity keep distressing thoughts at bay." This is what I did for most of my life. This is what most people do.

After you have done the work of differentiating yourself from your family of origin and the surrounding noise of your upbringing, you're ready for a second step to cultivating the inner life. Much like being scared of the dark or not going down to the dark basement, we scurry around on the same floor of the houses of our lives when there are second and third and fourth floors and a garden and a swimming pool and a basement.

It is in the basement that we find trinkets and useless tools and boxes of things we no longer need. We have shoved them there because it was too painful or we were too busy or distracted to go through the mess. So. We just put it on a shelf and get nervous if someone mentions that box on that shelf.

But this is the necessary step to deeper cultivation of your heart. Remember how we saw that the heart is the wellspring of life, where all other issues flow from? When we stay at the surface of conversation with others and never enter into conversation with ourselves, we are merely skimming the top of the water. It may look clean and pristine, but you know and I know that there is a dead body on the bottom. Do you drink from such a well?

This second step toward spiritual formation is akin to actually putting the clay on the spinning wheel. You set your intention of the kind of person you want to be—that you want to make a coffee mug. Not that you have to decide to actually enter the space and put the clay on the wheel and begin spinning.

Silence and solitude are not the same thing. Silence is simply turning off any outside noise you can. It is sitting in your room without music and without television and without notifications from your phone. I encourage those I coach with aiming for 10 minutes of silence. So that means putting your phone in Airplane Mode. Have a space where no one will talk to you (and you're not at risk of being talked to, because you will always be on alert. You have to know that you will not be interrupted. For those with babies and toddlers, that means you will need to be even more intentional about when you will do this. If you know nap time is coming at 1, then plan to have your 10 minutes of silence at 1:10-1:20.

I promise you. It sounds so simple, but it is a way for your soul to decompress all that has been compressed into your mind and heart. It is like defragmenting the hard drive of your mind and heart.

When I was in college, my computer would start to work more slowly and shut down programs randomly. I happened to live on a hall with a bunch of computer science guys who had built computers when they were in middle school. I asked them what's up, and they told me I needed to "defrag" my hard drive.

Essentially, what would happen as you used your computer, your short-term memory would remember partial pieces of information, and the longer-term storage would file things away next to other things that weren't related. It looked like a messy basement. Defragmenting your hard drive put like things together to make your processing more efficient. I think a better name would have been "reintegration". It took all the fragments and put them in order.

Many of us live fragmented lives. We hear a crossword here and an eye roll there at work, and we get home, and we interpret everything our family does with that same lens. A lens of performance and proving yourself at work into the home where unconditional love and acceptance should be the lens.

Silence helps us reintegrate our lives.

Solitude is a deeper and more intentional time. Whereas silence can be done with your kids in the next room, solitude requires you to get away. They often are talked about together because they go hand in hand. They are both after a similar result—self-awareness. Solitude is something you have to plan for in your calendar in the month. It is an extended time away from those same distractions we spoke about earlier. But it's for an extended period of time and often requires you to change your location.

I know people who take a day away each month to re-calibrate. They go to a retreat center and unplug from everyone and everything for 24 hours. Unavailable. No cell. No email. No television. No conversation. And sometimes no music. As you set on this journey, you will come to know what you need to do.

The important thing is that you get by yourself for an extended period of time. One of my favorite places to go is the cemetery. No one will bother you, and it's a great reminder of our mortality. It's quiet and provides space to think. You won't hear cars honking or people arguing in the next room or a business conversation happening at the next table at a coffee shop. Of course, these are ideals, and you may not be in a season of life where the ideals work for you. You do, however, still need to put the principle into practice. You may need to pay a babysitter for four hours once a month so you can get away.

Whatever you need to do, you have to set the clay on the wheel. Nothing happens by simply looking at the clay and imagining a coffee mug.

Fasting.

Oftentimes, my times of solitude are coupled with fasting. While I practice intermittent fasting for my health, it also serves as a spiritual discipline. But there is a difference between merely fasting and spiritual fasting. But the beauty is that you can do both at the same time. Most health advocates simply speak about the physical benefits of fasting—and there are myriad. But spiritual fasting is when you go without food so that you can fill it with spiritual reflection. Put another way, when you would normally eat, you fill that time with silence and solitude and reading and prayer and journaling.

When you feel the hunger pangs, press into that pain spiritually. Reflect on how you are a dependent creature and constantly need food, water, and air. Imagine the physical pain you're feeling is equivalent to the post-workout soreness. Don't simply wish the pain away. Sit in that pain and receive it as a gift.

Spiritual fasting also typically has an agenda. The agenda could be simply a cleansing of the soul. Your agenda could be a desire to break your addiction to pornography. It could be breaking the addiction to people's approval. Or something else you have identified as what are commonly called "besetting sins". These are hindrances to how you run your race in life.

As you sit in silence and solitude and consider cultivating certain virtues, you will see patterns rise to the surface. Maybe you're overly critical. Perhaps you're fearful of sharing your opinions. Maybe you spend money as soon as you get it. Maybe you never spend a dime. These are all indications of something deeper that you need to go down into the basement to look at…in all there musty and moldy glory.

I would recommend setting aside a 24-hour period each month whereby you do not eat anything. You only drink water and black coffee or tea. Perhaps you're saying, "Matt, I don't drink black coffee or tea." All the better! Force yourself to rid yourself of your comforts. Push yourself to do something that you typically do each day without thinking twice about it. You are forcing yourself to slow down.

In spiritual formation, slowing down is the secret sauce. In a world that measures our value by how much we do, these tried and true practices of fasting and silence remind us that our value is not dependent on our accomplishment. Rather, we are still loved and valued at the end of a fast and silent retreat. People still want us in the room. The temporary pain not only teaches you self-discipline and makes your body your servant, it cultivated gratitude. That first bite of food, whether it's a steak or a peanut butter and jelly, is amazing. That's what fasting fosters.

Reading.

One of the tried and true ways to be deeply formed is to have what is known as a spiritual guide. A mentor. Someone who is older or more attuned to the particular area you need help in. A financial advisor may not be older than you, but he has spent time studying and considering different vehicles in which you can invest your money. Akin to this is the Spiritual Advisor. Someone who has spent time reflecting on the inner life and has come back to help others.

As you spend time in silence and solitude and fasting, it is highly beneficial to read. To take something into your soul. I have found guides such as Henri Nouwen, Thomas Merton, Brennen Manning, St. Augustine, Bernard of Clairvaux immensely helpful in turning over the worn soil of my heart. Some don't read them because they are unknown in their circles. Others don't because they can't get past the emotive language. I would venture to say that that aversion is the *very* reason people ought to journey with them.

Other authors that can be helpful are Ralph Waldo Emerson, Henry Wadsworth Longfellow, Walt Whitman, Henry David Thoreau. The goal here in reading is to *slow down* (i.e., secret sauce) and consider the lilies of the field for a moment. To smell the roses or to wake up and smell the coffee. To get to the matters of the soul, you don't have to only read soul-directed books.

That approach is what I call going through the front door. You see an issue you want to tackle in your heart, so you pick up a book on that particular vice. For example, I am constantly trying to cultivate humility in my heart, so I will often take books written on humility—past and current.

If you are beginning to set out on this journey, I would encourage you to take the back door approach. That is, writers like Emerson, Whitman, and Thoreau spent countless hours reflecting on the beauty of the world and our place in it. They cultivated a heightened awareness of God's presence in the sky and mountains and trees and grass and sea.

What I want to encourage you to do is grow this awareness as well. I want you to be more aware of God's working through every bird chirp and breeze and then conversation (when you re-enter civilization). Due to our being accustomed to the noise of the world, our ears and eyes are deadened to the utter exploding effervescent involvement of the Creator of this universe.

This is not a treatise on the existence of God. There have been plenty of other authors who have given the requisite treatment of that.

As a Christian, I believe every human being has interwoven into their psyche a God-consciousness. That is, each of us knows that God exists, but we often distract or suppress that truth. Why?

There are so many reasons. But at a base level, it stems from each of us wanting to do what we want without being told what to do. We love our autonomy and don't want to depend on God to direct us because, in essence, we think we know better…and it is my life.

Perhaps you're in that place. There's no judgment here. But I venture to say you picked up this book because you wanted to cultivate your heart. You want to grow and change and know that your soul needs to be tended to. You know how to set SMARTER goals. You know how to reverse engineer. You know how to build systems. But you also know that there is a deep and abiding and vital and missing foundation. You've busied yourself with many things, while there is really only one thing needful…to know your Creator and to sit at his feet. He welcomes you to do that.

Without condemnation.

Perhaps you grew up in a hypocritically religious environment or an overly controlling and religious environment or a so-it-yourself and pull-yourself-up-by-your-bootstraps environment. All the while, you've known in your soul that "something ain't right" (as my Kentucky friends would drawl).

Those antennae that have gone up and that hair on the back of your neck or that pit in your stomach are all good things to be attuned to. Hypocrisy and spiritual abuse are heinous and worthy of condemnation. But don't let them keep you from the abundant life that Jesus promised to anyone that would come to him.

How do we know what he said? The Bible has been the trusted and reliable source for Jesus' words for close to two millennia. Even more, the Torah was the trusted text Jesus read. Like the existence of God, I don't have time to go through an explanation on the divinely inspired nature of the Bible. (See Resources at the end of the book for that). But I can promise you that in your developing of your inner life, the Bible is the preeminent source to go to.

If you're new to the Bible, I would suggest the following: Read one Psalm, one chapter in Proverbs, and one chapter in the Gospels—starting with Matthew. These three chapters will probably take you five to ten minutes to read. Read slowly. Circle ideas you don't understand. I would highly recommend getting a Study Bible. I would suggest the ESV Study Bible. It's a treasure trove of notes to explain hard-to-understand verses and concepts and has a lot of really good introductory articles to various topics of interest.

The key to reading the Bible is simply slowing down. Here are some general questions to help guide you in what to be reading for:

What does this text tell me about God?

What does this text tell me about me and my place in the world?

What does this text stir in me to do?

What is hard for me to understand?

Prayer.

What you read will inform how you pray. Prayer is a drawing near to God. It is characterized by talking to God. It is also characterized by God talking to you. You have heard from him in your devotional and Bible reading and silence and solitude. Now you begin to commune with God through prayer.

The word originally comes from the Latin *precari*, which means "to beg". This is one element of prayer, but I like it because it speaks to our need or desperation. When do you beg someone for something? When you really, really, really, really want something bad. Bad enough to look foolish and insignificant. Bad enough to where you are not concerned about what others think.

There's a woman named Hannah in the Old Testament who wanted a son so badly that she would often go to pray at the house of the Lord. One day as she was praying, the priest Eli thought that she was drunk. Here's what she prayed:

My heart exults in the Lord;
  my horn is exalted in the Lord.
My mouth derides my enemies,
  because I rejoice in your salvation.

2 "There is none holy like the Lord:
   for there is none besides you;
   there is no rock like our God.

3 Talk no more so very proudly,
   let not arrogance come from your mouth;
for the Lord is a God of knowledge,
   and by him actions are weighed.

4 The bows of the mighty are broken,
   but the feeble bind on strength.

5 Those who were full have hired themselves out for bread,
   but those who were hungry have ceased to hunger.
The barren has borne seven,
   but she who has many children is forlorn.

6 The Lord kills and brings to life;
   he brings down to Sheol and raises up.

7 The Lord makes poor and makes rich;
   he brings low and he exalts.

8 He raises up the poor from the dust;
   he lifts the needy from the ash heap
to make them sit with princes
   and inherit a seat of honor.
For the pillars of the earth are the Lord's,
   and on them he has set the world.

9 "He will guard the feet of his faithful ones,
   but the wicked shall be cut off in darkness,
   for not by might shall a man prevail.

10 The adversaries of the Lord shall be broken to pieces;
   against them he will thunder in heaven.

The Lord will judge the ends of the earth;
 he will give strength to his king
 and exalt the horn of his anointed.

There are three things we learn about Hannah's model.

First, there is a way of respect and honor as we approach God. Yes, we can pray to God whenever we want. But there is an element to how we approach God. Not in a chummy way, though he is a friend to those who develop that relationship.

Second, we acknowledge the ability, power, and goodness of God to meet the needs that we have.

Third, we submit ourselves to what God has for us and believe that because he knows our deepest needs and because he is good and because he is powerful, he will give us what is needful and good abundantly.

The beauty of prayer is that it stems from an acknowledgement of our inability. So often we spin our wheels trying to fix ourselves or others. It is gloriously true that God has given us agency in the world. But when you consider how little you control, it can be overwhelming.

You cannot control others' thoughts about you, no matter how hard you try. There will always be someone who misinterprets what you do or say. You can't control the weather or the airlines or the traffic or your job promotion or your co-worker or spouse or children or cats. Sure, you can work to persuade. But ultimately, you can only control your thoughts and actions. And as you get older, the amount you control of your actions diminishes.

Prayer, then, is a willing surrender and looking outside yourself for help. There is something very therapeutic about opening your hands. In fact, when I pray, I often pray with open hands as a physical representation of an inward reality.

Along with this physical posture, it is a good idea to have a plan that will guide you through. You could use the Lord's Prayer. This has been done for centuries and has proven a great support in cultivating your inner life:

> *Our Father in heaven, hallowed be your name, 10 your kingdom come, your will be done, on earth as it is in heaven. 11 Give us today our daily bread. 12 And forgive us our debts, as we also have forgiven our debtors. 13 And lead us not into temptation, but deliver us from the evil one.*

You can also use other resources like the Book of Common Prayer.

There is also great benefit to praying from things that are from your own heart. As you grow in this discipline, here's an outline that can get you started:

L: **LISTEN** to his Word and declare your **LOVE** for God. That he is your King and Friend and Father.

I: Tell him the **ITEMS** and **IDEAS** that you're working through. Start with items you're grateful for and move into those which you need him to help you.

F: Commit to live by **FAITH** in however and whenever he chooses to answer your prayers.

E: **EXCLAIM** his worth and your desire to find ways in which you can **EXERCISE** that faith in him in your daily life.

Journaling.

Now that you have begun to cultivate a life of prayer, the next step in turning over the ground of your heart is the discipline of journaling. There have been scientific studies done that show when we journal there are neural connections being made that would not otherwise be made by merely thinking about something.

I have found that the depth of my experience in prayer and meditation and throughout the day was greatly improved when I started journaling. My mind is constantly turning over ideas or conversations I had that day and I can seem to be swirling in a sea of thought…completely drowning. Every time I begin journaling it is like I am throwing my scattered and swirling brain a life raft. It is easy to get overwhelmed with feelings, never quite sure why we are struggling.

When I set pen to paper—and I do recommend a pen not a pencil… the Pilot G-2 or Schneider One Business—I force myself to think through my emotions. I often will simply do stream-of-consciousness writing with no filter just to get thoughts out of my head.

Other times, I follow a simple plan of processing. If you are new to journaling, try it every day for one week. As you reflect on your day and your thoughts, you will look back in hindsight and see that you had more clarity and were better able to understand your circumstances and interactions with the world.

You can get the following template and a lot more practical tools by signing up for My New Rich Life—where you'll get the Workbook that has them. Go to www.MyNewRichLife.com

For now, just use the next page to journal for today. Feel free to simply use these questions to help you in your journal. They help you consider how you are interacting with the world around you. So often we just go from event to event and never reflect on how we're feeling or felt. We don't slow down long enough to consider if I could have shown up more of myself to that moment.

We say we value certain things, but if people were to look at the actions of our lives, they would be hard-pressed to find proof that it's all that important to us. These journal prompts will help you walk through the various areas of your life to do the work of reflection and set intentions.

Date & Time:

What is on the front of my mind:

What have I eaten today:

How do I feel physically?

      1   2   3   4   5   6   7   8   9   10

What conversations have I had today:

What has brought me joy or relief today:

What has frustrated or disappointed me today:

Is there anything I would do differently today:

Service to others.

When it comes to forming our inner lives, very little thought is given to our interactions with the world around us and how it can help our souls.

When I was in high school, I battled depression and suicidal ideation for a few years. Through those years of private battling, I was in my own head. Every conversation I had, I reflected on how I sounded—"Did I sound stupid when I said that?"; "Does that person like me?" Every assignment, I reflected on whether I got the highest grade. Every presentation, I wanted to make sure people knew I had studied and was smart. I was constantly worried about how people perceived me.

Maybe that's you too.

A lightbulb went off, though, when I was working at a local YMCA. I had initially started volunteering there to build my college resume. One day, I began to realize that my spirit had lifted throughout the day because I was intrigued by the youth I was serving. I didn't worry if I sounded weird or if they thought I was smart. I enjoyed conversation for the simple enjoyment of it. Simply enjoying getting to know the person I was talking to.

If you find yourself in a spiritual slump, I want to encourage you to think of one person you can call and encourage. If calling is too much, just send an encouraging text letting someone know what you appreciate about them. Go ahead. Do it now.

So many spiritually dry people are spiritually dry because they have become very self-focused and they never realized it. Others are cynical about others and judgmental. I knew this one man who had been religious for fifty years, but he was the most unpleasant person I had been around. He was constantly putting off the vibe that he was better than others—that he understood what was right and wrong and others had no clue. That his convictions were the right ones. Needless to say, this person is very isolated. He doesn't have anyone speaking into his life because he is, quite frankly, repulsive.

As you consider the kind of person you want to be, every virtue (or character quality) is strengthened through relationships. In fact, in a key interview in My New Rich Life, my counselor Dr. Jim Cofield shares this very overlooked element to our spirituality. Our relationships are the garden from which our character grows and is nourished.

Consider this. If you wanted to be a kind person, you would want to encourage others. Imagine, though, that everyone around you was sarcastic and cut each other down. You tried and tried to be a better person, but every time you tried they would make fun of you.

Have you ever heard of the crabs in a bucket phenomenon?

One day a fisherman noticed on the pier a man who was catching crabs. He would pull up his crab cage, pull them out, and throw them in a bucket. As the fisherman observed him, he drew closer in fascination. As he got within a few feet he noticed the bucket had no top on it!

"Say, why don't you have a top on the bucket?! Won't the crabs crawl out?"

"I ain't worried. Just watch."

Sure enough, the fisherman watched, and he noticed a very peculiar thing. Every time a crab would get to the rim of the bucket, he would fall back down. But as he watched longer, he noticed that the crab wasn't falling down…he was being pulled down.

This is the case with each of us as we seek to improve our lives. As you try to improve who you are, people (both intentionally and unintentionally) will seek to keep you at their station in life. If you surveyed the five closest people in your life, you would probably find that you all make around the same amount of money and have the same kinds of jobs and have the same kind of pastimes and the same level of fitness and health. Of course, there are exceptions to this rule, but it's generally true.

Whether people want to admit it or not, they do not like people in their circles doing better than they are financially. Unfortunately, people put their self-worth in their paycheck. But it goes a little deeper than that, to be honest. And this is the wonder of My New Rich Life. When you begin to level up your fitness and your discipline, you will see your finances improve. You will be more disciplined in your spending because you have learned the beauty of delayed gratification.

As it pertains to serving others, consider your immediate circle of five people. Who is one person you could encourage today? Who is one person you could begin practicing the virtue of goodness with? As you practice being more encouraging, you will be more encouraging. Sound funny and pretty straightforward? It is.

We overcomplicate our spiritual lives to think that it's about being an ascetic. But in our day, it is not the call for all of us to isolation and a vow of silence. Rather, it is utilizing the relationships as tools for your inner growth.

Dark side.

Psychologist Carl Jung challenged the then-popular notion that our psyche was a series of simple chemical reactions. Against Skinner's behavior modification, that highlighted the part of our human consciousness as largely unconscious, action-reaction living, Jung spent time considering the spiritual and ephemeral side of our being. Of particular note was his work on the "shadow side."

I like to call this the "dark side," in homage to Star Wars. I believe Star Wars paints a very clear picture of each of us facing in life between light and dark. Between who we project to be and what we hide from others. The self-control we exhibit while people are watching contrasted with the indulgences we enjoy if we think no one is watching. The reason why the drama for Luke Skywalker persisted for three episodes (and three more for his dad in the prequels) is due to the persistent and omnipresent nature of the darkness we wrestle with.

What Jung is helpful with, though, is instead of taking up arms against the dark side, it is beneficial to our wholeness to ask what the draw of the dark side could tell us about ourselves. I counsel many, many people who try to deny their darker inclinations. They are often surprised when, instead of moving onto the next thing, they will spend time asking clarifying questions about those inclinations.

Let's be honest. Every single one of us has thoughts and desires we're not proud of. They could be lustful, self-righteous, proud, jealous, anxious. You name your own that, if everyone knew about it, you would clam up in horror.

What I want you to do, though, is to make amends with that dark side.

I have seen people spiral down into not-so-good tendencies and places (including myself), because they were too embarrassed of those things (or things).

That shadow side, that dark side, is part of you. You want something because you see a lack. Just as we do a lot of self-editing when we're at a dinner party, so also we do ourselves no favors when we stuff that darkness down.

The more therapeutic answer is to talk with that dark side of who you are. Do you need help to know how to do that? While this kind of guidance is best done face-to-face, because I want to help, I will risk it. And go ahead and write them here in the book.

The following questions will begin to train you to do what is sometimes called "shadow work". It is work because it will require of you a level of reflection and honesty that most people never want to do. It is shadow because it not only works on the shadow side of who we are, but it can often be elusive. Don't let the difficulty of the questions frustrate you to not do the work. It is worth it...

The thing I am most ashamed of in my thought life is:

I am afraid that if people knew this about me, they would:

I am entertaining those thoughts, because I really want:

If that desire were met, I would know/have:

Hard Side—Avatar of the Intense Self.

One of the most unbelievable stories of recent years is that of Navy Seal and Army Ranger and ultra-marathoner, David Goggins. Now, if you have sensitive ears, you will not want to read or listen to his two books (or podcasts)—as every other word is the f-bomb. I will say, his story is inspiring. He was not always in amazing shape. He did not always exhibit such mental resiliency.

He was abused as a child and saw his mother and brother abused by his father. He was constantly being told he wouldn't amount to anything of value. He had a learning disability. His home life was utterly broken. He was in horrible health and living an aimless life.

One of the things that began to shift in his mindset was when he developed an alter ego he simply calls "Goggins". Essentially, this is a harder side of who he is. Similar to the dark side, the hard side differs in that it has a resiliency to it—a toughness.

Each one of us has this more resilient side. We just may have never trained ourselves to tap into it.

You may have felt this surge of confidence in a moment you didn't expect it. Perhaps you experienced it when things seemed horrible and you couldn't see any way out. Maybe you were in a difficult conversation and when you would typically shut down, you spoke up. When your boss said that annoying comment and belittling one too many times, you had had enough and said something. You felt it.

You need to tap into that resiliency. In becoming more familiar with this resiliency, you will be able to bring it to the surface more readily. You will be able to strengthen a muscle that has always been there; it just hasn't been exercised in a long time.

Here are some questions to help you tap into that hard side. And yes, go ahead and write your answers here in the book:

What is an extremely difficult time I went through in my life?

Did I get through it? Yes or No

How?

What did I learn about myself through this difficulty?

Emotions chart.

One of the things that high achievers, and those focused on their personal growth, is that we are often not very self-aware or self-reflective. As such, when people ask me how I'm doing, if I want to be honest and true, it takes me a minute to ask. I spend a lot of time thinking about the future (and the past), but struggle to live in the present moment.

I am critiquing the past (as Ones on the Enneagram often do). Or I am planning the future (as Eights do).

One of the tools that has helped me tremendously is something so elementary (in fact, don't they put these in elementary schools?!) is an emotions chart. I gravitate towards only a few emotions if left to my vocabulary, and someone asks me how I'm doing. I'll either be happy, angry, or sad.

Having an emotions chart helped me tremendously to have a vocabulary for how I'm actually doing. You will see on the chart I'm sharing to help you on the journey of deeper and more meaningful self-awareness and emotional health that "happy," "angry," and "sad" are the core emotions...but there is a plethora of nuance that you can use to help clarify how you're doing and, by extension, how you're doing.

On the next page is an Emotions Chart. If you're like most people, when asked how you're doing you probably say "fine". If a trusted friend asks you, and you have more than a 30-second assessment, you might say something like "tired" or "overwhelmed" or, the all-too-popular and entirely unhelpful, "busy". These are not really states of being. They avoid the *how* in the question and settle for the *what* are you doing.

Many marriages struggle because couples never learn how to communicate *how* they are actually doing. The Emotions Chart will give you a more expansive vocabulary so that you can develop honest dialogue around *how* you're doing. You can get one online or just carry this book around. The key is to actually look at the words and use them.

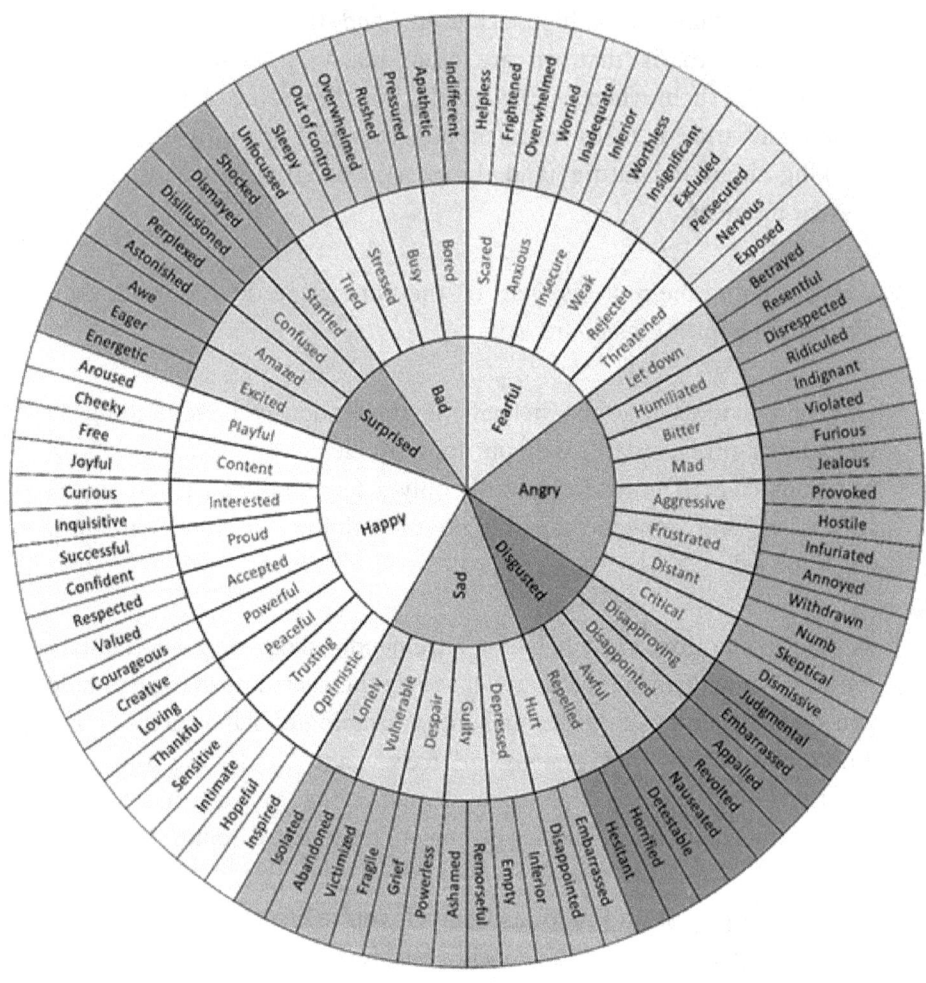

So...

How are you doing in this moment?

Use the next page to free flow write it out. Believe it or not, this may be the most therapeutic thing you do this week. But, like with most things in this book, you have to actually do the work. So...go ahead...write down: "How are you doing?" Or better: "How are you feeling?" And then, "Why?"

Boundaries Make You Free

We often equate boundaries with purely limits and don't consider that without limits there can be no flourishing. Think about a garden. If you didn't set boundaries for certain vegetables, they would get all entangled and damaged by encroaching vegetables. If you didn't put a fence around the garden, deer will come and have a feast. If you didn't till the soil and set a hedge around the garden, weeds would soon take over.

Look at any ghost town that doesn't have the repetitive action of cleaning and repairing boundaries and you will see a disheveled place.

One of the guilty pleasures is to watch time lapse videos on Instagram of overrun properties get cleaned up and put in order. One of the first things they do is chop away the overgrowth before they get into the fine work of putting lines in the yard with their precision mower.

I know. It's strange…but apparently I'm not the only one who likes these videos—easily garnering millions of views.

In his book, Discipline Equals Freedom, Jocko Willink says, "Motivation is fickle. It comes and goes. It is unreliable and when you are counting on motivation to get your goals accomplished—you will likely fall short." So many times we believe that we just need to get motivated to lose weight. Or when we do get motivated to lose weight and we're on Day 20, we get frustrated that we aren't losing as much weight as we thought we should.

When I speak about boundaries, I am also talking about discipline. That word has been woven throughout this book. What you and I need to get our new rich lives…our changed lives…we need discipline.

Instead of saying, "I'm not allowed to get a second plate of food." Say "I don't get second plates of food." You see how your boundary of not getting a second plate is wedded to your identity of who the new you is?

The former way of thinking is an external boundary that will yield no discipline to actually follow through. By connecting your boundary with your identity and then devoting yourself to being the kind of person you want to be, you will have success. It's when you listen to the siren calls of cutting corners or fudging the lines that you lose touch with the person you want to be.

There's another aspect of boundaries that you need to understand if you are going to get the abundant life you want.

You are going to have to embrace your own finitude. You constantly need something. You're not self-existing. You breathe. You eat and drink. You are a dependent being.

So much of my life has been marked by not heeding my boundaries and running after success that always seemed elusive. I would commit to a certain path. Look to my left or right and see someone be successful in something else...and then I'd change course. I had come to believe the false notion that I could do it all.

When you and I can embrace and appreciate that we can't do it all, we can actually get to a place of excellence.

The spiritual practices I taught in the previous chapter work that muscle of accepting your finitude. When you are silent, you are in the passive/recipient place. You are listening; you are not running but sitting still. When you are fasting, you have to feel the hunger pangs and be reminded that you can't keep yourself alive.

As this reality is driven deeper into your psyche, you begin to feel relief that you will never get all your to-dos done. God is the only one who does get his to-do list done.

I have to remind myself of this reality daily. I am naturally geared to get things done. I love getting things done. This is a good trait, and I'm glad I have it. But, like all good traits, there's a shadow side to it so that it becomes the identifying piece of my self-worth puzzle. That is, I can feel defeated or less than if I don't get much accomplished.

As a result, I can often feel frustrated or fearful. Frustrated that something still hangs over my head. Fearful that I will never be able to get that important thing done.

By reminding myself of my finitude—my boundaries—I actually begin to find contentment. I begin to slowly remember that I do not keep the world rotating.

Anxiety is kept at bay in another way that has been groundbreaking for me. By having my boundaries, I have to ask myself if something is mine to do or if that is in someone else's orbit. Brian Tracy has said, "You cannot control what happens to you, but you can control your attitude toward what happens to you, and in that, you will be mastering change rather than allowing it to master you."

Stoic philosopher and former slave, Epictetus, said much earlier

> *The chief task in life is simply this: to identify and separate matters so that I can say clearly to myself which are externals not under my control, and which have to do with the choices I actually control. Where then do I look for good and evil? Not to uncontrollable externals, but within myself to the choices that are my own... (Discourses, 2.5.4–5).*

Imagine that. He knew better than anyone else that he did not control what he ate that day or if he ate. Where he went. What tasks would be given to him by his master. But it was in his slavery that he learned the power and beauty of boundaries. Controlling what he could control.

This goes into the very practical realm of how people treat you. You can only control how you operate and present yourself in the world. You alone determine what you will do with the lot that has been given to you. You didn't control who your parents would be. You didn't control how horribly that person treated you. You didn't control that referee that made the wrong call. You only control your thoughts and actions.

When you get a hold of that, your joy increases. Your freedom excels. You don't have to change the world. Leave that to God. All that you have to do is be the person of integrity, self-control, charity, and virtues that you want to live.

You need to continually ask yourself:

Is this mine to do?

    OR

Is this situation in my control?

If it is, then set your hand to the plow and get to work. If it's not, then kick your feet up and breathe in deep.

Do you struggle with how people think of you? Guess what. Not yours to do. As Andy Mineo raps:

If you don't like me, that's your problem.

When I let it bother me, that's my problem.

And as he says in another place:

If nothing changes before I'm gone,
I got no one else I can blame it on.
And we've been waiting way too long.
What if we're the ones that we're waiting on?

What freedom comes to your life...what abundance...when you remember that what people think of you is not yours to deal with. Your reputation matters, sure. Be honest. Be kind. Be truthful. Be gracious. But always remember that even the perfect example of such a life was crucified.

Along with this concept of boundaries is the need to reinforce your boundaries. I do not use illicit drugs. If I were around someone who was trying to force me to take them, I would simply slap his hand away. If they persisted, I would simply leave. This is upholding my boundaries... and by extension, my boundaries.

As Gandhi said, "I will not let anyone walk through my mind with dirty feet."

We spend inordinate amounts of money protecting our possessions. We have security systems, pay monthly for alarm surveillance, pay monthly insurance premiums all to protect our stuff. But how much energy and effort do you expend to protect your person? People ask you to hang out, and you really don't like their company…but you do it anyway. People gossip about a co-worker and you know you shouldn't but you fail to uphold that boundary and a flood of cesspool water pours into your ears and heart.

I love people. I love learning their stories. I love cheering them on to success. This love for people can sometimes get me into trouble.

For example, I have given people relational access to my heart—my fears and anxieties and besetting sins—but they had not earned the right to hold those very precious parts of who I am. As a result, they dropped them and abandoned me in the process. The pain was searing. It cut deep. And I was left reeling and wondering what was wrong with me.

I had not practiced appropriate transparency. Not everyone you meet has the right to all of you. You are an amazing person with beautiful qualities that can bless so many. Out of respect for yourself, do not be so quick to give the most intimate parts of who you are to everyone.

You must know your boundaries and reinforce those boundaries when people threaten to cross them. You will be treated how you let people treat you.

Do you wonder why another boyfriend is talking down to you? Because you're letting him. You are a beautiful creature made in the image of God…you simply need to remember and act in accordance with that truth. Tell him your boundary. If he violates it again, walk away. Yes, it will be hard. But if you don't respect your boundaries and reinforce them, then you are giving him permission to own you. Please. Don't. Do. That.

It is often said that your five closest friends will largely determine the kind of person you will be. If you take an inventory of the people around you—the five people you spend the most time with—are they the kind of person you want to be? Do they gossip about others and put their other "friends" down in your presence? They will do that to you when you're not in the room. I promise. That's who they are. Does your circle constantly talk negatively or have a fixed mindset and castigate anyone who would try to change? Yep. You'll be them in a very short amount of time and long forget the principles of this book.

A word of caution. Deciding to uphold your boundaries will prove to be very lonely at times. As you are more careful and judicious with who you let influence you, you will find that there are very few people who fit the bill. At least initially. But over time, like attracts like. Your intimate circle of one or two friends will multiply. But you must respect your boundaries and not let others determine who you will be.

Your New Rich Life

Okay. This is it! It has been necessary to lay all this groundwork because the last thing you want to do is come away with a whole lot of to-dos and life hacks without the virtue and character formation that will enable you to remember why you're hacking in the first place.

As I mentioned, one of the biggest things I saw lacking in the personal growth space is the formation of the interior life we spent so much time in the previous chapter honing. Even in the Mental and Physical chapters, I sought to connect those elements of your being with a deeper and more lasting understanding of your personhood.

You can think positively but succumb to feeling compelled by powers and societal standards outside of you. If you work diligently to clarify the kind of person you want to be, you will capture not only the positive thinking but it will be interwoven into your inner being so that you, eventually, don't have to think about cultivating that virtue. It will simply be who you are.

You can be the most disciplined person in the gym, but your relationships are a wreck. Over time your insides are eaten up through stress and worry so that you waste away on the inside and then on the outside. After all, consider how many illnesses are traced back to a broken heart or an anxious soul.

You can spend your entire life climbing a ladder…only to realize that the ladder was leaned against the wrong wall.

How many people have purchased a bill of goods that they need to go to college, get a good-paying job, get a nice house with a nice yard, and retire on a golf course?Nothing inherently wrong with any of these things. They are simply the result and ought not to be the goal.

A rich life is the result of a rich mind, body, and soul.

A rich life is an integrated and whole life that doesn't suffer from disintegration.

A rich life is a life well-lived in harmony with others and harmony with yourself.

A rich life takes intention and care.

The rich life is living by your values

A Carrot or A Stick.

A famous proverb says that the best way to move a donkey is by dangling a carrot in front of him. This is a reward.

You can also get a donkey to move by a punishment of hitting him in the hindquarters with a stick.

Unfortunately, these two ways are the only two ways people have identified to get themselves moving. At a very primitive level, these work. But as a creature made in the image of God, you are more than reward and punishment. There is deep within you a longing to be what God fashioned you to be.

Unlike the nihilist who believes we are a collection of haphazard particles that just happened to come together at some unspecified point millions (or is it billions?) of years ago. We are not a protozoa turned tadpole turned whale turned ape turned man. This is a huge leap of faith.

Even more, there is no grounding for why you ought to be better if there is no design or purpose to this story. Sure. You can make it up how you want, but the question still remains unanswered in the closed system of pure materialism.

Of course, I don't have time to go into a wholesale explanation of meaning and ethics in this book.

I bring it up to merely underscore the fact that you are not the result of happenstance. You were created. You were fashioned for more. You have been born at this particular time in this particular place to read these particular words with a particular purpose to tell you that you matter in this hurling globe of spectacular precision.

As such, you have embedded within you a longing. Perhaps even a pulling or a pushing that originates from without but reaches deep within your psyche on those moments of silence and solitude.

God wants you to experience a rich and abundant life. As Jesus said, "I came that they may have life and have it abundantly." The image here is that of a cup overflowing. In that overflowing, others are able to have their cups filled. And this continues forever.

You are intimately connected to this earth and are interwoven into the lives of others. How are you showing up in the world? Are you just getting by or are you effecting change and blessing for others?

Next Steps.

You have started that journey and are so much further ahead than a majority of the population. You have not only identified areas of growth, but you have also taken the practical step of getting help.

Please don't be like I was for most of my life. I simply acquired more information and life hacks but never implemented them.

Implementation is the next step in your journey.

I'm serious.

Too many people think that knowing is all there is to a rich life. Some call it "want-trepreneurship"—where people want something different but fail to see the mundane and unnoticed work necessary to actually be someone different.

Right now, you're a want-er. I want you to be a do-er and a be-er (ha!). In doing the things we've identified and related here, you will begin to be a different, more integrated person. You will bring your best self to the party. You will see that you were created to make a difference in other people's lives. You will see day after day the beauty and wonder and glory of giving your new rich life away to others.

The story of the Bible is that God blesses people not so that they can simply buy nicer houses and nicer cars. To spend their wealth only on themselves...but, as God said to Abraham, " I will bless you so that you can be a blessing to others." Indeed, the entire world!

That's what I've been aiming for in this entire book. I want to free you from living for the applause of others. From being a slave to their opinions that keep you trapped from being all that God created you to be and do.

Yes. It's safer to watch the latest Netflix series. But was Tiger King really worth it?

As John Shedd famously quipped: "A ship in harbor is safe, but that is not what ships are built for."

You were created for more than what you're living for now, friend. You may be living your best life now...but what is the criterion you're using for that measurement? What is more...Are you providing room on your boat for other people to enjoy that rich life with you? That is the key identifier for your new rich life. Are you living wide open and welcoming and generous?

Vision.

The first NEXT STEP is to consider a personal vision for your life. You have been fearfully and wonderfully made. Made for a specific purpose. A calling. And God is calling you into that beautiful next act in a cosmic play. It will take courage. But that courage is fueled by a vision.

In an effort to get at that vision, I want you to take a moment to reflect on these questions to then write a clear, one-sentence personal vision statement:

What brings you joy in life?

When you look at the world around you, what is one thing you get angry about…that you would like to see changed?

The last time you laughed was?

The last time you cried was?

In light of the previous moments, what do you seem to enjoy doing the most?

If you had a week to yourself and could do whatever you wanted (excluding a vacation-like existence), how would you spend your week? What would you do?

What have people asked you for advice on?

What do you feel most natural doing…as though the sun is shining on you and time slows down?

I want to live the rest of my life:

BIG FIVE

In my coaching program, My New Rich Life, I have folks send me a list of their Big Five. These are the five areas they want to focus on. While I spend a lot of time walking them through how to determine their 10-year, 5-year, 1-year, 90-day, and 30-day Big Five in the areas we've covered in this book: Mindset, Physical, Spiritual, I want to help you a little in your own journey.

Consider for a moment the kind of person you want to be (your vision). And consider where you want to be one year from now in each of the three areas listed below.

Mind

1)

2)

3)

4)

5)

Body

1)

2)

3)

4)

5)

Soul

1)

2)

3)

4)

5)

From that vision, what habits and practices do you need to implement *now* for those things to be true of you?

Consider what you can do these next 90 days and consider the habits you want to cultivate *today*. But only pick five from that list of fifteen. These are your Big Five for the next 90 days.

My Big Five:

1)

2)

3)

4)

5)

Accountability.

Okay. Now you are getting clearer on the kind of person you want to be. Hopefully, you did the above exercise. It is worth knowing the kind of wall you want to set your ladder against.

But vision and motivation alone will not get you where you want to be. You need 2-3 people who believe in you to hold you accountable to living the kind of life you want to be dedicated to. List those people out here:

1)

2)

3)

You need to call each of the above people and share with them what you've been contemplating and writing. You have a deadline for this. You need to call each of these folks within the next three days. Stop now and put who you will call on each day for the next three days.

Community.

Friends are nice to have, but sometimes they will go easy on you. The NEXT STEP you need to take is to be part of a community that will call you to your better self.

This book is a clarion call to such people.

I felt compelled to write this book because I wanted to gather people together who have felt this calling, but have not heard someone blast it aloud...yet. You need other people in your life who will push you and prod you and pull you. Push you to the best version of yourself. Prod you to a greater existence. And pull you to that next summit in your life.

You may be in a small town similar to the one I grew up in. You may find it difficult to find people who have a desire to be better today than yesterday.

You may be in a big city that overwhelms you with finding like-minded people.

You may be in a larger town…but a comfortable town like the one I currently live in, where stability is the mark of a well-lived life. BUT you want more from these 80 years you have prescribed for you on this earth.

You want abundance and riches in relationships, in finances, in mindset, in health, in your soul…and you want that abundance and wealth so you can share it overflowing. You want your cup so overwhelmed with these gifts that they spill out into others' lives.

Sign up!

It would be wrong of me not to give you the opportunity to join a growing group of like-minded people in the program I have been mentioning throughout this book.

I was slow to write this book and put together My New Rich Life because I am afraid of self-promotion. And that has been a mistake. That fear has been to a fault. Sure. It's good to be slow to puff out your chest and pretend that you have all the answers. That you are the guru.

But that fear can be wrongly debilitating, as my coach Dan Long has reminded me time and again: "If you have a gift for the world, it is wrong for you to keep it."

My New Rich Life is my gift to the world.

A call to all of you to your best self. Your higher self.

Let's join together on this journey together in personal growth. I don't have it all together...But what I have, I want to share with you. And I want to delight and share in the gifts you were created to bring into this world.

Next Steps

FREE 30-Minute Coaching Call

FREE Resources

My New Rich Life

Emotional Intelligence Quiz

Since you purchased the book, I want to give you some next steps...and at a discounted rate. If you click through the QR codes above, you'll be taken to some special discount pricing for the various programs and a free coaching call so we can help you start defining and implementing the things you've learned in this book. It's free. What do you have to lose? You've already spent the time and energy to get this far. I would hate for you just to let it remain as information. Knowledge alone is not power. It is knowledge applied that makes a difference in the world. An idea is a beginning. But everyone has ideas. It's those few people that actually do something with that knowledge that change the world...

I can't wait to see what amazing things you do in the world!

About the Author

Matthew Wireman has been committed to serving others to become all that God created them to be. With over twenty years of coaching and counseling all over the world, Matt loves to help people who are committed to being the best version of themselves today—instead of waiting to do something tomorrow. He currently serves as Program Director of Christian Ministries Online at North Greenville University and is the founding pastor of Christ the Redeemer. His greatest joys are his wife and four children. They have been the greatest catalysts for Matt's own transformation and growth through love, acceptance, and belief.

You can follow along in his own journey of self-discovery and growth at www.MatthewWireman.com

www.ingramcontent.com/pod-product-compliance
Lightning Source LLC
Chambersburg PA
CBHW050640160426
43194CB00010B/1751